DISCOVERING
HISTORIC AUSTRALIA

Jan Gleysteen
1210 Loucks Avenue
Scottdale, Pa. 15683

DISCOVERING
HISTORIC AUSTRALIA

DOUGLASS BAGLIN/BARBARA MULLINS

Editorial Assistant MARGARET MARTIN

Designed by
BERYL GREEN

URE SMITH • SYDNEY

Front jacket: Glenrock, near Marulan, N.S.W., convict-built of golden limestone with fluted columns cut all in one piece. It was the home of George Barber, who first settled in the district in 1821, but it is believed to have taken many years in the building and was probably not complete until around 1840. Barber married Isabella, sister of Hamilton Hume, and Hume and Hovell stayed at Glenrock on their journey of exploration to Port Phillip in 1824. Glenrock was restored in 1965 and is classified by the National Trust.

Preceding pages: Simple cairn of stones marks the trig station at Seal Rocks Point, Myall Lakes. Seal Rocks, off the central coast of N.S.W., are a cluster of rocky islets about midway between the mouths of the Hunter and Manning rivers. They are a haven for seals and a hazard for mariners, and, after considerable indecision about where it should be sited, a lighthouse was finally completed on the neighbouring headland in 1875.

Glen Helen Station, in central Australia. One of the earliest cattle stations in the area, it was established in the eighteen-eighties by pioneer settler Fred Raggatt, who ran the first general store in Stuart (now Alice Springs). This is Namatjira country, daubed with the colours from his pallet. Glen Helen gorge, with its towering red cliffs and deep waterholes, is one of the few permanent watering places in the area.

This page: Trademark of pioneer Australia — stockwhip, hand-plaited from bush-treated hide to the individual requirements of the stockman, and hand-stitched saddlebag. The stockwhip is essentially an Australian development, devised to meet the special needs of the Australian bush. Skilled hand leatherwork such as this is still a feature of many outback stations. Lumley Park, N.S.W.

Following page: Old timber shearing shed at Jindabyne, N.S.W. This is the country of which "Banjo" Paterson sang: the original "Man from Snowy River" is claimed by some to be "Hellfire" Jack Clarke of Jindabyne. The old bush-timber structures of pioneering days, honest and simple in design, are at one with their surroundings; they blend in a way that is the envy of modern-day architects.

Back jacket: Grave of John Flynn, at the foot of Mount Gillen near Alice Springs, is marked by an eight-ton granite boulder from the Devil's Marbles, a remarkable natural formation in central Australia. John Flynn, "Flynn of the Inland", pioneered the Royal Flying Doctor, a unique aerial medical service covering two million square miles of the Australian continent.

First published in Australia, 1974 by
Ure Smith, Sydney
a division of IPC Books Pty Limited
176 South Creek Road, Dee Why West, 2099
Copyright © Douglass Baglin (photographs)
Barbara Mullins, Margaret Martin (text) 1974
National Library of Australia Card
Number and ISBN 0 7254 0211 3
Designed by Beryl Green
Printed in Hong Kong by Toppan

acknowledgements...

The authors wish to acknowledge the great debt they owe to the poets and bush balladists of Australia, both those whose lines are quoted in this book and the many others who proved a constant source of inspiration.

The lines introducing The Seekers are from "Sea Chronicles" by Rex Ingamells, those introducing The Settlers are from "The Pathfinders" by Vance Palmer, the introduction to The Builders is from "Old Botany Bay" by Mary Gilmore, to The Battlers, from "Country Town" by Judith Wright and the lines introducing The Dreamers are by D. H. Lawrence, who spent a period in Australia in the 1920's; they were applied to William Lane, visionary and poet, in Lloyd Ross's biography: "William Lane and the Australian Labor Movement." The couplet quoted on page 50 is from "The Broken-Down Squatter", the verses on page 53 from "The Sheep Washer's Lament" and those on page 55 from "The Eumerella Shore", all are old bush ballads. The verses accompanying the illustration of the ruins of the old convict settlement at Norfolk Island (page 118) are from "The Old Prison" by Judith Wright. The contemporary account of Ben Hall (page 123) is from the selection, Colonial Ballads, by Hugh Anderson; "The Ballad of Ben Hall", quoted on page 125, is an old bush song. Verses from Henry Lawson's "Past Carin" accompany the illustration on page 124. The verses quoted on page 126 are from "Biami" by Kath Walker, and those on page 130 are from "Namatjira", also by Kath Walker. The lines from Henry Lawson's "Song of Southern Writers" (page 134) are from Marjorie Pizer's collection of his works: "The Men Who Made Australia". The authors also wish to extend sincere thanks to Rachael Roxburgh who introduced them to a number of the old colonial homes of New South Wales.

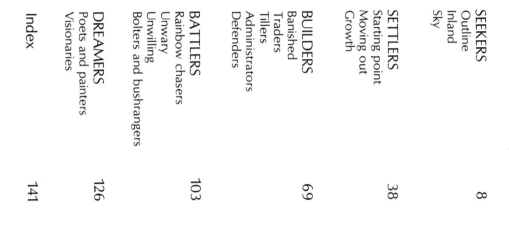

contents...

*Where old-time ships came, canvas seagull-white
articulate around our coast, the seas
speak sailors' Spanish, Dutch and Portuguese,
mutter and roar and whisper, day and night . . . .*
—Rex Ingamells

Seekers

Though the vast southern continent of Australia lay uncharted for centuries it is impossible to believe that its coasts had not been sighted and its shores littered with the graves of strayed ships. Chinese junks made extensive sea voyages in the 15th century, gathering bêche-de-mer and other delicacies — surely their harvest grounds included the Great Barrier Reef. Japanese traders combed most of the Pacific seeking the fragrant white sandalwood prized in the Orient for more than thirty centuries; their ancient maps show parts of a coastline that could be Australia's. Inca legends tell of rich lands lying west of South America. Malays spoke of the great land to the south that was the home of their dead. The Greeks, who knew that the world was round, believed there might be a Great South Land. Some say the sailors of ancient Egypt ventured to its shores. In the Middle Ages it was unknown yet sketched vaguely on the map — mushroom-like beyond the barrier of fire that was the equator. Myth and legend grew. The great land of the south, it was told, held an unbelievable booty in gold and spices — if only it could be found! Dutch, Portuguese and Spanish expeditions set off in secrecy hoping to track down the El Dorado. Gradually its outlines — and gaps — began to appear on mariners' maps; strange distorted outlines to today's eyes, but to the eyes of four centuries ago, the key to a treasure house of long-guarded secrets, a booty of wealth!

They were, of course, preceded by many thousands of years. The first seekers to reach Australia were the Aborigines, believed to have travelled from Asia along a string of islands aeons ago when rising and receding seas of the Ice Age formed fleeting land bridges. They carried back no tales of its secrets, but took possession of the vast empty continent. For thousands of uninterrupted years they adapted themselves to the country until they became part of it. Then, in a few short centuries the tranquillity of the last of lands was shattered. Strange white sails of spirit ships loomed on the horizons as the great south land took form in European eyes and was pulled slowly into the net of western civilization.

Buccaneer Archipelago, named for British buccaneer William Dampier who landed somewhere in the vicinity in 1688, is one of the most treacherous areas on the Australian coast, marred by violent rips and whirlpools, scene of numerous shipwrecks, known and unknown. Dutch mariners of the early seventeenth century, running before the westerlies across the Southern Ocean, sometimes overran their turning point and made landfall, if not a wreck, on this forbidding, reef-strewn, rocky coast.

6

The Dutch were the first Europeans know[n] to have seen Australia, and Duyfken Poin[t] on the western shore of Cape York Peninsula, is the scene of the first recorde[d] landing. The Duyfken (Little Dove), commanded by Willem Jansz, left Batavia [in] November 1605 to explore New Guinea [and] made landfall on the Australian coast in March, 1606. Jansz reported: "We found nothing but wild coasts, barren land" inhabited by "wild, cruel and barbarous savages" (they murdered some of his crew[). This report stopped further Dutch investigation for at least a decade.

Dutch sea captain Frederik Houtman, instructed by the Dutch East India Compa[ny] to follow up earlier reports of the unknow[n] southern continent, sailed up the west co[ast] of Australia in 1619, and sighted, among other places, the reefs and islands now known as Houtmans Abrolhos (a term wh[ich] translated roughly, means "open your eye[s"]. Scene of many shipwrecks, they amply justified the warning. First and most notorious was the wreck of the Batavia in 1629. Mutiny and massacre followed the shipwreck, and the crude stone barricades built by those survivors who refused to jo[in] in plans for piracy, still stand to this day.

First Dutch captain to bring back a description of the west coast was Dirck Hartog, on Eendracht, in 1616. He left a record of his visit on a pewter plate, nailed to a post on the island later named for hi[m]. It remained there until removed by compatriot Willem de Vlamingh in 1697 (h[e] replaced it with one of his own). After som[e] wanderings, Dirck Hartog's Plate, the oldes[t] relic of European contact with Australia, is now in the National Museum, Amsterdam. The Vlamingh Plate was in turn removed b[y] French explorer Louis de Freycinet in 1818 and taken to Paris. It was returned to Australia in 1947, after being mislaid for mo[re] than a century, and is now in the Museum and Art Gallery of Perth, together with this replica of Dirck Hartog's Plate.

The Dutch were also the first Europeans to record the southern coast of Australia. Pieter Nuyts, Dutch navigator, was on two occasions blown onto the southwest coast of Australia. In 1622, in Leeuwin, he explored the area around Cape Leeuwin; in 1627, on Gulden Zeepaard (Golden Seahorse), first ship to enter the Great Australian Bight, he ventured as far as the archipelago which now bears his name. Bruni d'Entrecasteaux, in 1792, searching for the lost La Perouse, described the cliff formation as "an aspect so uniform that the most fruitful imagination could find nothing to say of it." Matthew Flinders surveyed the area in 1802 and commended Nuyts' charts; Edward Eyre tramped the area by land, from Adelaide to Albany, in 1840, and described it as a "desolate and forbidding" region.

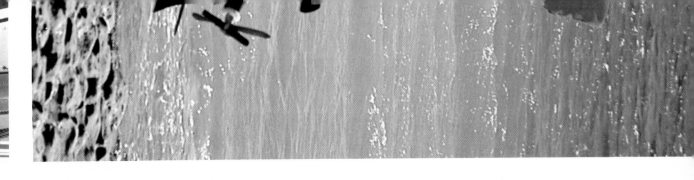

outline...

By some strange paradox early mariners in search of the continent stumbled upon many of the numerous islands which dot the Pacific but missed the enormous land mass of Australia. English mariner Francis Drake, in his circumnavigation of the world sailed south of Timor and must have been close to our coast. Spaniard Pedro Fernandez de Quiros, inspired by the Pacific voyages of countryman Don Alvaro de Mendana, led an expedition which made landfall on an island in the New Hebrides. Quiros firmly believed that this was the great south land, and joyfully gave it the name of *Australia del Espiritu Santo* — "Australia of the Holy Spirit". (The spelling of "Australia" was in honour of Phillip III of Spain who was a prince of Austria.) Luis Vaez de Torres, a member of the Quiros expedition, was separated from his commander and sailed south west hoping to find the real "Terra Australis"; he was within two hundred kilometres of the Barrier Reef when he gave up hope of sighting land and turned north toward the Philippines. He planned to sail along the east coast of New Guinea but was forced westward and found himself picking his way through the dangerous waters of the strait which now bears his name. Perhaps he even sighted the tip of Cape York Peninsula and dismissed it as an island!

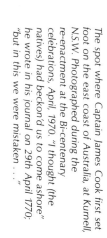

The spot where Captain James Cook first set foot on the east coast of Australia, at Kurnell, N.S.W. Photographed during the re-enactment at the Bi-centenary celebrations, April, 1970. "I thought (the natives) had beckon'd us to come ashore" he wrote in his journal on 29th April 1770; "but in this we were mistaken . . ."

Journal of Sir Joseph Banks, open at the pages describing the escape from Cooktown.

Coral-encrusted cannons jettisoned from the Endeavour in 1770, recovered in 1969 after lying for nearly two centuries beneath the waters of the Great Barrier Reef. After cleaning the cannons proved to be in remarkably good condition; the coral growths, up to four inches thick, had inhibited corrosion and the gunfounders' markings and embossed monogram of George II were clearly visible when the coral layer was removed and the surface stabilised.

In view of the Spanish activities in near Australian waters it is surprising that the honour of the first recorded sighting of the continent by Europeans should go to the Dutch. The *Duyfken* (Little Dove) under command of Willem Jansz sighted Cape York Peninsula and sailed down its western shore into the Gulf of Carpentaria. She anchored near what is now the Wenlock River and a boat was sent upstream. Hostile contact was made with the Aborigines (a Dutchman was killed). The first shaking outlines appeared on the map.

The next section to be filled in was the west coast. Dutchmen Dirck Hartog (1616), Jacobsz (1618), Frederik Houtman (1619) all added their bits to the jigsaw. These were ships that had been blown to the east from the Dutch seaway across the Indian Ocean to the Spice Islands. Slowly the Dutch filled the gaps on the western and northern parts of the map. They were still in hope that the inhospitable land they saw might hold Marco Polo's "Beach" with its fabled wealth of gold and spices. First sighting of the east coast was by a Dutchman, Abel Janszoon Tasman, in his ship *Zeehaen* (Sea Cock) in 1642. He skirted Tasmania, naming it Van Diemen's Land, and his voyage proved that the South Land stretched from Cape York around the partly known west coast to the Great Australian Bight, possibly even as far as Van Diemen's Land. No trading possibilities had emerged and the Dutch began to lose interest in "New Holland". However they had given the continent a shape, and charted shores now replaced fantasy. The British completed the outline.

When Captain James Cook set out from England in 1768 ostensibly to make astronomical observations in the Pacific, he was secretly instructed by the Admiralty to search for the great southern continent: "If you discover the continent . . . employ yourself diligently in exploring as great an Extent of the Coast as you can. . ." his instructions read. "You are also with the Consent of the Natives to take possession of Convenient Situations in the Country in the Name of the King of G't Britain. . ."

14

Careening Place, Endeavour River, north Queensland, where Cook's damaged Endeavour was careened and repaired after running onto coral reefs near Cooktown. Cook described the area as "extreamly convineint for heaving a ship down" and it is still used for that purpose today.

His primary mission, to observe the 1769 passage of Venus over the "Disk of the Sun" complete, Cook sailed southward, circumnavigated New Zealand, and then resolved to "steer to the westward until we fall in with the East Coast of New Holland . . . and than to follow the direction of that Coast . . . until we arrive at its northern extremity." Cook sighted the east coast of New Holland on April 19th, 1770: "The Southernmost point of land we had in sight . . . I have Named it Point Hicks, because Leuitt Hicks was the first who discover'd this land . . . the sea shore is all white sand," he wrote in his Journal. The ship anchored in Botany Bay on April 29th; Banks and Solander collected plant specimens and made brief excursions inland. Eight days later Cook was on his way northward again, coming near to disaster when the Endeavour floundered on a coral reef but succeeding in bringing back to England the results of his carefully carried out explorations. The map was now almost complete; it remained for Flinders to circumnavigate the continent and fill in the few missing links.

In 1796 Matthew Flinders, with George Bass, established that Van Diemen's Land was an island and made "our long-wished-for discovery of a passage into the Southern Indian Ocean". Between 1801 and 1803 Flinders, in command of Investigator made the first coastal circumnavigation of Australia, charting the shores with great skill, thoroughness and persistence. The outline was now complete. The South Land left the realms of legend and became a reality, whose known shores now beckoned men to the unknown interior.

Endeavour Reef, north Queensland, where the Endeavour went aground in 1770. Cook described the area as " . . . surrounded on all sides by dangers . . . quite at a loss which way to steer . . ."

Actual specimen of Hakea gibbosa collected by Banks and Solander at Botany Bay in 1770. This is one of a number of Banks' specimens, which survived the grounding of the Endeavour on the Great Barrier Reef and the journey back to England, and are now in the possession of the National Herbarium, Sydney. The area was originally called Stingray Bay, but Cook later wrote in his Journal: " . . . The great quantity of New Plants &c Mr Banks and Dr Solander collected in this place occasioned my giveing it the name of Botany . . ."

Captain Cook's watering place, Kurnell. It was from this small pool that Cook's party found sufficient fresh water for their needs.

Cooma Cottage, Yass, N.S.W., home of explorer Hamilton Hume, built about 1830. A skilled bushman, Hume, with his brother Kennedy and later William Hovell, was responsible for opening up much of southern New South Wales.

Lower right: Detail of exterior, Cooma Cottage. The building is classified by the National Trust.

inland...

A century of inland exploration revealed a diverse and contradictory land — rolling grass plains, fertile valleys and mountain ranges of breathtaking grandeur shared the continent with endless stretches of waterless desert, perilously rugged horizons and the windblown wastes of the Great Australian Bight. The earliest land explorers were cautious and reasoned; their goals were immediate — land was needed for farming and later to support the colony's ever-increasing flocks of sheep. Later exploration was tinged with rashness and dare-devilry. The men who arrived with Governor Phillip and the First Fleet must have pondered on the nature of the vast unknown country that surrounded the tiny settlement. "Botany Bay", as it was generally known, had been chosen for a penal colony because it was a natural gaol — and indeed the first colonists were imprisoned on the shores of Sydney Cove. To the west lay a barrier of mountains; the country to the north and south, crisscrossed with rivers, could contain any number of unknown perils.

Explorers' Tree, Katoomba, N.S.W. This tree was marked by Blaxland, Lawson and Wentworth on their historic first crossing of the Blue Mountains in 1813. This important relic of the early days of Australia has unfortunately suffered at the hands of vandals and from the ravages of time; it is now dead and in danger of rotting away despite attempts to preserve it.

Mount Blaxland; from this peak Blaxland, Lawson and Wentworth surveyed the new-found pastures of the west, before returning triumphant to Sydney.

Carclew, at Monteforte Lookout, South Australia; starting point for Sturt's gruelling expedition to the centre.

Sturt's Tree, Fort Grey, in the frightening Corner Country where three States meet. Sturt established a depot here for his inland explorations; the tree bears the inscription "Sturt 1845".

The first tentative inroads were made by Governor Phillip, pushed by the need to find more suitable farming land than was offered at Port Jackson. He travelled north to Broken Bay and named an inlet, Pittwater, for the Prime Minister of England. His travels up the Parramatta River led to the development of a farming district at Rose Hill, and he explored the Hawkesbury River. The first white men to travel the coastal strip of south eastern Australia were survivors from the *Sydney Cove* wrecked near Preservation Island, Bass Strait, in 1797. Seventeen men reached the mainland in a long boat and then set off to walk five hundred miles up the coast to Sydney. It was to take them three months; only three survived, the first white men to gain knowledge of that long strip of coast. One, the super cargo, W. Clarke, kept a graphic diary describing the country and the rivers they had to cross.

For twenty-five years the colony edged outward, but expansion continually ran up against the impenetrable wall of the Blue Mountains. Under the influence of John Macarthur, flocks of sheep soon spread over all available grazing land east of the ranges. The situation was aggravated by the effects of drought and plagues of caterpillars. Overgrazing of some parts of the country meant that sheep quickly cropped the best grass before it had a chance to seed and pastures were being rapidly over-run by less appetizing coarser grasses. The dry summer of 1811 followed by the spring rains of 1812 intensified the army of caterpillars which destroyed crops and further depleted grazing pastures. Sheep became the driving force for exploration. New grazing land had to be found if the wool industry was to prosper. Necessity turned eyes to the blue barrier rimming the west. Gregory Blaxland and his brother John were among those whose stock had suffered. Disgruntled by the rejection of their repeated requests to be granted additional land (Governors Bligh and Macquarie felt that the brothers were "discontented, unreasonable and troublesome" and not using their land to the best advantage — that is, agriculture) Gregory Blaxland, in 1813, accompanied by two other stock-owners, William Lawson and William Charles Wentworth, tackled the mountain range in the hope of finding new areas for their flocks and herds. In the course of earlier excursions in the area west of Cowpastures, Blaxland had developed a theory which was to crack the towering mystery of the mountains. They climbed to the plateau, keeping "the streams of Water River" (Warragamba) on their left hand, and "the Streams of Water which emptied themselves into the River Grose" on their right. The journey along the ridges was slow and arduous, paths had to be hacked through the dense bush and food and water for the horses was a constant problem. After sixteen days the party reached Mount York mountain where they tasted grass for the first time since they had left the other side of the range. The explorers

crossed the Cox River and reached Mount Blaxland before turning back. Their mission had been successful. They had found "forest land . . . sufficient to feed the Stock of the Colony . . . for the next thirty years." Men and sheep streamed across the ranges and the frontiers of the colony were rapidly pushed back. Venturers such as Evans, Oxley, Mitchell, Hume, Hovell, Cunningham, Strzelecki and McMillan carried out recognised exploration in the name of wool. Flocks followed them south west to the Riverina and the Monaro Plains, crossed the Murrumbidgee and the Murray and reached as far south as Port Phillip. In the north the Liverpool Plains, the New England district and the Darling Downs gave up their fertile secrets. These were the official explorations. The unsung explorers were the ever alert men who kept one step ahead of the official parties, claiming waterholes, staking out their runs and quietly moving in their stock. The country west of the mountains proved reassuringly familiar. There were no lost cities or pathways to China (as had been fondly imagined by convicts seeking release from the rigours of the settlement). However it did hold one great mystery — the resting place of the waters which its rivers carried purposefully westward, strange rivers that seemed to flow the wrong way, into sands and not seas. Where did they go? Was there an inland sea? Did they cross the continent to the north west where they might open up settlement and trade with Asia? In 1817 John Oxley set out to follow one of these rivers, the Lachlan. His party were soon bogged down. "The whole country . . . was either complete marsh or lay under water . . ." Oxley despairingly recorded. "It is impossible to imagine a more desolate region . . . I much fear that we shall not be able to proceed much further . . ." Oxley split his party and with three men persevered down the Lachlan only to be blocked again by vast swamps. A further two days' journeying would have brought him to the Murrumbidgee but Oxley turned back: ". . . it was with infinite regret and pain that I was forced to come to the conclusion, that the interior of this vast country is a marsh and impenetrable. . ."

The inland rivers remained a puzzling problem. The marshes that had frustrated Oxley did not lay the theory of an inland sea, but rather encouraged it. In Captain Charles Sturt's opinion it could still be there. ". . .The ocean of reeds which had proved so formidable to Mr Oxley formed most probably the outskirts of it. . ." he opined. In 1828, leaving behind an undistinguished soldiering career, Sturt led an official expedition up the Macquarie River to prove "whether these conjectures were founded on fact." It was the beginning of a long and far-ranging journey for Sturt, for not only was he to solve the riddle of the rivers; he was to go on to cover and discover vast tracts of the inland of the continent.

The old Mount Poole Station, near Milparinka, N.S.W., an early sheep station now derelict. Sturt's party camped near here in 1845 on their way to the Stony Desert that now bears his name. They had set out from Adelaide hopefully seeking good land in central Australia, but were imprisoned here for nearly six months beside a dwindling water supply, the only remaining source that they could find.

Aerial of Mount Poole shows the intolerable country which claimed the life of James Poole, Sturt's second-in-command. He died from scurvy and exhaustion in July, 1845, within days of the breaking of the drought that had held the party prisoners through searing summer heat and the bitter cold of winter.

With Sturt on his first expedition was the experienced explorer, Hamilton Hume, who, four years earlier with William Hovell, had travelled overland to Port Phillip, finding rich grazing land. Sturt and his party, travelling in a year of drought, walked on dry, caked earth skirting the marshes which had baffled Oxley. Fresh water was a constant problem and it was with delight that they finally came to the banks of "a noble river" — a delight that quickly turned to bewildered despair. "The men eagerly descended to quench their thirst," wrote Sturt. "Shall I ever forget the cry of amazement . . . or the looks of terror and disappointment with which they called out to inform me that the water was so salty as to be unfit to drink!" (This was because of the drought.) They called their new find the Darling; it was the first link in the solution of the puzzle.

The following year (1829) Sturt once again set out to solve the mystery. This time he traced the Murrumbidgee to see whether it ended in marshland, joined the Darling, or found its own way to the southern coast. The party followed the river until brought to a standstill by marsh and beds of high reeds. Sturt however felt that the Murrumbidgee continued as a river, and his decision to proceed by boat was confirmed by a group of Aborigines who told him of another waterway to the south ". . . to which the Murrumbidgee was but a creek, and . . . we could gain it in four days . . ." They did indeed reach a junction. ". . . I cannot describe the effect of so instantaneous a change of circumstances upon us," Sturt joyously recorded. "The boats were allowed to drift along at pleasure, and such was the force with which we had been shot out of the Murrumbidgee, that we were carried nearly to the bank opposite . . . while we continued to gaze in silent astonishment on the capacious channel we had entered . . ." They had reached the Murray River.

After an eventful journey on this river they were joined by the waters of "a new beautiful stream" — the Darling! The riddle had now been largely solved; all that remained was to discover where the Murray emptied its waters. This, they found, was "a beautiful lake, which appeared to be a fitting reservoir for the noble stream that had led us to it." Sturt named the lake Alexandria, after the young princess who was to become Queen Victoria. His travels had taken him overland across the corner of the continent. He had unravelled the mystery of the rivers; they drained into the Darling and the Murray, and finally into the southern sea. Sturt returned nearly blind, but after a period of recuperation in England was once again drawn to Australia. He made one of the first overland journeys with stock and in 1838 was appointed Assistant Commissioner of Land for the newly established settlement at Adelaide. It then became his obsession to be the first to reach the centre of Australia; he was convinced that it contained good grasslands and perhaps even the elusive inland sea.

This stone cairn was built by Sturt and his weary men as a surveyors' mark and to keep themselves occupied during their enforced stay at Depot Glen (Mount Poole). Poole died shortly after its completion, and Sturt dedicated the cairn as a memorial to him.

Poole was buried under a beefwood (grevillea) and the tree was marked with his initials and the date of his death. Later a stone pillar was erected beside it. The party had been trapped there for months, after exploratory probes in all directions had revealed only barren land and dried-up waterholes. In the first months the heat was so intense they sought to evade it in an underground chamber gouged out of ground which Sturt recorded was "thoroughly heated to a depth of three or four feet". In the following winter months they were forced to build a chimney into their underground refuge so that a fire could be lit for warmth.

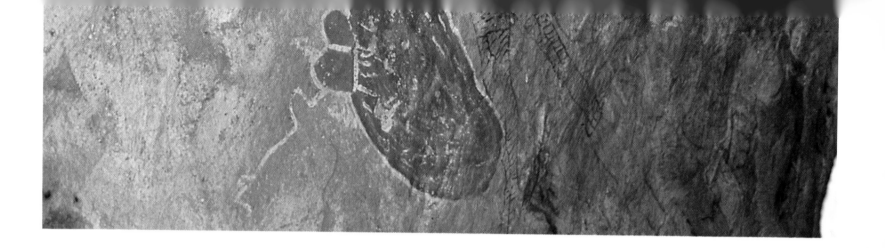

With envy he watched the departure of Edward Eyre who, enacting Sturt's own dream, headed north into the interior. Eyre's expedition was largely unproductive in terms of useful land and in 1844 it was Sturt's turn to lead a party into the inland. The expedition followed the Murray and Darling rivers to Lake Menindee and then branched north west, making camp beside the water supply at Depot Glen. Here, hemmed in by drought and temperatures which averaged 38 degrees Celsius, they were forced to spend six months. The next base camp, Fort Grey, further into the north west corner of New South Wales, was the stepping stone used by Sturt to make him two extensive journeys into the centre. These took him into Lake Blanche, across the Stony Desert and along the banks of Cooper Creek. The country he crossed was a patchwork of extremes; barren sand ridges gave way to grasslands which in turn changed to stone-clad plains. Sturt returned to Adelaide on January 19th, 1846, leaving his second-in-command, James Poole, buried near the mountain that now bears his name. His travels had taken him seventeen months and although he had not reached the centre of the continent or found the hoped for expanses of grazing land he had released many of the geographical secrets of the Australian interior.

The exploration of Australia, although carried out in often intolerable conditions, was in the main accomplished without loss of life. But the tragedies that did occur stand out, a testimony to the recklessness of the unlucky adventurers, overshadowing explorations which were brought to a successful conclusion. Kennedy, Leichhardt, Burke and Wills rank among those who did not return. In 1848, after two journeys of exploration in the dry west, Edmund Kennedy turned his attention to the far north. Preparations gravely underestimated the difficulties; the men had to face dense jungles in an area which had the highest rainfall on the continent and was home to tribes of hostile Aborigines who savagely resented the intrusion of the white men. The party was landed at Rockingham Bay — "a viler looking country never looked me in the face before", Kennedy confessed. His orders were to travel overland to Port Albany on the tip of Cape York, where he would be met by a ship. The four hundred cruel miles this involved were to claim ten lives, including Kennedy's. The Aborigine, Jacky Jacky, and two starving men plucked from a depot, were the only survivors.

The unsolved mystery of the disappearance of Ludwig Leichhardt's second expedition in the interior of Australia has remained the great puzzle of Australian exploration. The party of seven men and 77 animals were never seen or heard of again. Search parties brought back fragmented tales gleaned from the Aborigines — the men had mutinied, they had been killed by Aborigines, survivors were living with tribes as wild white men — but the mystery has never been solved. Despite several claims not one relic of the men or animals of the expedition has ever been recovered.

This Aboriginal painting in a cave near Cooktown, Queensland, is believed to be a record of the tragic Kennedy expedition of 1848. Kennedy had hoped to reach the tip of Cape York Peninsula, but after months of constant hardship and attacks by hostile natives, was fatally speared as he neared his goal. Six members of his party died of starvation and three others suffered an unknown fate.

Yet the challenge of the interior remained hard to ignore. The expedition which next took up the gauntlet carried Burke and Wills to their death. They set out to cross the country from south to north. The leader, Robert O'Hara Burke, was a police inspector. William Wills, twelve years his junior, joined the expedition as astronomer and surveyor. Neither had any experience of exploration and their knowledge of the bush was limited. It was a prestige project, government sponsored; its aim was to enhance the reputation of Victoria and put that colony ahead of the others in the drive to the inland. The party left a festive Melbourne amid public fanfare, with the cheers of crowds ringing in their ears — an elaborate cavalcade, doomed to disaster and death in the sun-scorched wastes of central Australia by inexperience, mismanagement and hasty planning. Crowds greeted them as they moved through the settled areas and the goldfields before heading inland; letters pursued them from the Victorian Exploring Expedition Committee (which was financing the journey) urging them to move faster — Stuart was setting out from South Australia in the same direction, and the honour of crossing the continent must not be snatched from Victoria. Much of the twenty-one tonnes of baggage and supplies that trailed behind the convoy was auctioned off as the impossibilities of carting it across the interior became obvious. Slowly the expedition which was to end with its leader dying of thirst and starvation in the solitude of the inland, was stripped of its grandeur. A depot was established at Menindee and here Burke quarrelled with Landells, his second-in-command, who quit the expedition. His position was taken by Wills. Burke, in a party of eight men, pushed ahead to Cooper Creek, where they waited five weeks for the rest of the expedition before their impatience took control. Burke and Wills, with King and Grey, then pressed further on towards the northern coast. It was a hasty and ill-judged move. They did indeed beat Stuart in being the first to cross the continent from south to north for Burke, after once again splitting his party, raced on with Wills and one horse until he sighted the tidal waters of the Gulf of Carpentaria, but Gray died before they could regain the security of Cooper Creek. This was but one link in the chain of misfortune and mismanagement which dogged the project. When, ill and half-starved, the three survivors stumbled into the camp at Cooper Creek, it was to find that Brahe, who had been left in charge, had abandoned the depot only hours before. Food had been left at the base of a tree marked "Dig"; Burke recovered this and left a note in its place, telling the relief party of his decision to head for Mount Hopeless. He patted down the dirt after burying the letter and the relief party, thinking the ground undisturbed, failed to find it and assumed the party had not returned.

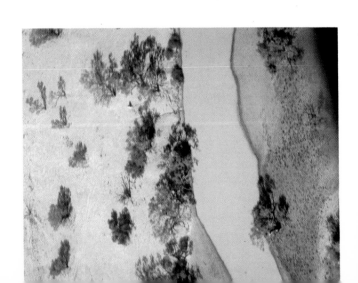

Aerial of the Cooper Creek depot of Burke and Wills, showing the famous "Dig" tree. It was from here that they decided to "dash into the interior and cross the continent at all hazards".

Mark made by Burke and Wills outside their room at the Menindee Hotel, N.S.W.

The Dig Tree, Cooper Creek, Queensland — mute witness to a tragedy of errors.

Grim profile of McLarty Ranges, Western Australia. This arid landscape is typical of the country traversed by explorer George Grey (later Governor of South Australia) in 1837-39 and by the Gregory brothers in the 1850's.

Chambers Pillar, central Australia, is a sandstone monolith first sighted by John McDouall Stuart in 1860 and named by him for James Chambers, who financed the expedition. It is perhaps better known as Explorers' Rock for it bears the carved names of many trail-blazers of the period.

For a time the weakened and starving men were assisted by Aborigines, who showed them how to pound Nardoo seeds into a form of flour, but death was inevitable. Wills, the weakest, begged to be left behind. Two nights later Burke died. King was given succour by Aborigines for two months, until found by a rescue party. The expedition had ended in appalling disaster. It had, as Burke reported in his Cooper Creek message, "discovered a . . . route to Carpentaria" but it had paid in lives. They had travelled too fast to collect useful scientific data; the search parties compiled far more valuable information on the interior.

John McDouall Stuart was a stubborn and determined Scotsman who three times attempted to cross Australia from south to north before his efforts finally met with success. Stuart had been a member of Charles Sturt's inland exploring party and had learnt much of the arts of survival and leadership from his old master. In 1858, using only a pocket compass, he covered 24,000 kilometres, discovering Chambers Creek and treading the rich opal fields of Coober Pedy. Stuart's dream was to cross the continent from south to north and to stake out some of the rich pastures he had seen for himself. In March, 1860, prompted by the £2000 reward the South Australian Government offered to "the first person who will succeed in crossing from this colony to the shores of either the north-west or the northern portion of the Australian continent . . . (and find) . . . the most practicable route for the overland telegraph . . ." Stuart set out again. On April 22nd he was able to record "today I find . . that I am now camped in the centre of Australia" and he named Central Mount Sturt in honour of his former leader (the name was later changed by others to Stuart). Haunted by ill health and harassed by Aborigines he finally turned back but did not give up. He was bitterly disappointed when a further attempt made in April, 1861, also failed, but in October of the same year he was on the track again. It was a gruelling journey and Stuart's health deteriorated rapidly; his eyesight was failing and he was weakened by hunger, fatigue and scurvy. On 24th July, 1862, his determination was rewarded. "The sea" rang out the call of the advance rider; "I dipped my feet and washed my face and hands in the sea" wrote a jubilant Stuart. The flag of triumph was hoisted and then, as recorded by Auld (a member of the expedition) "Stuart . . . seemed to collapse and said 'I have tried all my life to do this, and have now succeeded'.

After that Stuart went about as if he had no ambition in life . . ." Stuart was so ill on the 3000-kilometre journey back to Adelaide that he had to be carried on a litter slung between two horses for much of the distance. Though he received the £2000 reward for his epic journey, and a large lease of land, rent free, in the north, he never recovered his health to enjoy it. He returned to England and died there, four years later. His journeys had proved that an overland telegraph line was feasible and they made possible the development of central and northern Australia.

Though the shores of the west were the first to be sighted by white men, the land behind them was the last part of the continent to give up its secrets. Exploration was costly and the greener hills of the east had a greater claim on the attention and lives of Australia's explorers. The first determined probes were made in the late 1830's when J. S. Roe, Surveyor-General of the newly-formed colony at Swan River, opened up much of the country around Perth. Captain (later Sir) George Grey led two harrowing expeditions north to the Kimberley district, discovering rich pastures inland from the present port of Geraldton and bringing back sketches of fantastic Aboriginal paintings. A. C. Gregory followed, tracing the Gascoyne River (discovered by Grey) and locating further pasture lands. His later explorations linked and built upon the work of earlier explorers, contributing much to the knowledge of the north. In 1861 impetus for exploration in Western Australia came from a strange source, the American Civil War; Frank Gregory was sent to look for country suitable for growing cotton. Major Peter Warburton, with camels, made an arduous crossing of the interior from east to west in 1873. John Forrest later sought a more practical route across the deserts. But perhaps the most determined of the east-west crossers was Ernest Giles; success came on his third attempt and he then turned round and journeyed back to the east! By the late 1870's the continent had been criss-crossed by the tracks of explorers. It was the end of an age. Overlanders investigated the patches in between. It was left to aerial surveys to reveal the last mysteries.

The homestead of Angus McMillan, explorer, cattle trader and pioneer of the Gippsland area, near Sale, Victoria, the fertile region he discovered in 1839. McMillan "squatted" in the area and was one of the first to ship cattle from there. He was renowned for his protection of the local Aborigines, his hospitality and his public spirit. Unfortunately his homestead is now forgotten.

Cabin at Belltrees, near Scone, in the Hunter Valley of N.S.W., built by explorer William Charles Wentworth. Wentworth acquired the Belltrees property from the original owner, Robert Semphill, and later sold it to James White, in whose family it has remained since.

32

Vickers Vimy aircraft flown by brothers Ross and Keith Smith on the first England-Australia flight in 1919 (they took 28 days). The plane is on display at Adelaide airport.

Memorial to the "Southern Cross" — Kingsford Smith's famous plane — at Brisbane airport.

Victoria Hotel, Darwin, resting place for many of the famous international epic pilots.

Home of legendary Australian aviator, Charles Kingsford Smith, at Double Bay, N.S.W.

Home of Charles Ulm, Dover Heights, N.S.W.

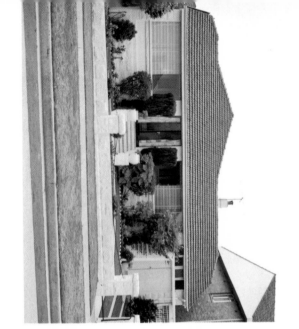

Sky...

Australia has always been an air-conscious country. The first short flights carried space-shrinking promises which were eagerly pushed to fulfilment. The great distances which separated the scattered population within the country, the expanses of rolling oceans which isolated the continent itself from the familiar cultures of England and America, could be conquered! Building upon the developments in aviation made during World War I, Australia was once again home to pioneers — men exploring a new and exciting form of transport.

The breathtaking days of races and record-breaking flights burst upon Australians in 1919. Ross and Keith Smith took up the Commonwealth Government's challenge of £10,000 made "with a view to stimulating aerial activity . . . . for the first flight to Australia from Great Britain . . . by Australians". The Smith brothers made the flight in a twin-engined Vickers Vimy (nicknamed "God 'Elp All Of Us!" after its registration letters GEAOU) through foul weather and over inhospitable terrain and landed on "Terra Australis . . . 27 days, 20 hours after taking off" to claim their prize. They had shown that a regular mail and passenger service by air between England and Australia was possible. Another great year was 1928. "Lone Eagle" Bert Hinkler, who later died in an aircraft crash in the Apennines, made the first solo flight from England to Australia in a light plane — "Hinkle, Hinkle, little star, fourteen days and here you are!" cheered the jubilant crowds. Charles Kingsford Smith and Charles Ulm, flying in the "old bus" *Southern Cross*, conquered the last barrier of the Pacific, linking Australia with the U.S.A. They then made a non-stop flight from Melbourne to Perth and crossed the treacherous stretches of the Tasman Sea to New Zealand. In the same momentous year they founded an airline company, Australian National Airlines (not connected with the A.N.A. which was later taken over by Ansett) but the disappearance of the *Southern Cloud* early in 1931, which carried the crew and eight passengers to their death in the Snowy Mountains, coupled with financial difficulties, spelled doom for the company. The loss of the plane (the wreckage was not located until 1958) was a severe setback to civil aviation. Mistrust grew as the dangers of air transport became apparent. Both men died with their dreams. Ulm was lost over the Pacific in 1934 and Kingsford Smith vanished near the coast of Burma in 1935. In each case they were attempting to set new records.

The almost impenetrable green jungle of the McPherson Ranges, northern N.S.W., scene of an air disaster in 1937, and a reminder of the perilous nature of the early days of air transport in Australia. Two survivors spent ten harrowing days in this dense jungle. They were near death when miraculously rescued by bushman Bernard O'Reilly who, following his own theory on the location of the missing plane, had forced his way through tangled growth "as tough as wirenetting" for two days before stumbling on the wrecked plane. Visibility was so poor it was "like travelling in a dense fog" he recorded, "and you can navigate by reckoning only." He did not see the plane until he was within a few paces of it.

Humble beginnings of the Australian international airline, QANTAS. This early hangar of the Queensland and Northern Territory Air Service stands at Longreach, Queensland. The first regular air service, from Charleville to Cloncurry, started in November 1922. In 1934 Qantas began its international flights.

Hangar of Connellan Airways, Alice Springs. Founded in 1939, this airline operates a unique service for people living on cattle stations, missions and mines in the remote areas of northern Australia. It is known as "the flying mailman".

The first attempt to develop air transport on a commercial scale was made at the end of 1921 when Western Australian Airways commenced operating a regular service. Kingsford Smith flew the deserts for Western Australian Airways before starting his own venture. The company had a relatively short and initially troubled career — an inaugural flight ended in a fatal crash. The early pioneering airlines were a product of necessity, an answer to the isolation of the inland. The Queensland and Northern Territory Aerial Service (QANTAS) was established in the central western Queensland town of Winton, and its first regular passenger service, in 1922, operated between Cloncurry and Charleville. By 1930 its planes had flown one million miles and a year later (with Imperial Airways) the airline ran an experimental mail service between England and Australia. In 1934 the flights were extended to Singapore; the outback airline was now international and took the name of QANTAS Empire Airways.

At the outbreak of World War II all parts of Australia were linked by airlines. England was only two days away and air mails and air travel were a firmly established reality. Air transport had removed Australia's isolation from the rest of the world and revolutionised life in the outback, bringing not only fast transport but playing a vital role in bushfire control, crop-dusting and cloud-seeding. Combined with developments in radio, it made possible the unique "Flying Doctor" service, which commenced operations in 1928 — a vision pushed to fruition by a Presbyterian minister, Reverend John Flynn, who felt it "would make all the difference for the brave people of the bush". Today the service has over twenty planes and thirteen bases providing medical service covering nearly a third of the Australian continent.

Minds that outran the ancient doubts and fears
They blazed the track for legions following after
And bared new treasures to the hungry years . . .
—Vance Palmer

Settlers

In the tracks of the seekers came the settlers; those who made Australia their own, who struggled to subdue the new-found continent. Willing or unwilling, they had endured uncomfortable sea months to reach the colony of limitless land. The forced settlers of the First Fleet were faced with an overwhelming and despairing task — carving a foothold on the edge of an unknown continent. Survival was a constant battle. Their tools were pitifully inadequate. Iron hard trees broke hearts and handles. There was not a plough in the settlement to break the untouched soil. Men became beasts of burden, dragging hoes in the savage heat of the upside-down seasons. Very few knew even the rudiments of farming. Misused tools were blunted and broken, or deliberately lost by convicts smugly providing themselves with an excuse for idleness. Much of the seed spoiled on the voyage and what was left produced a scanty harvest. Governor Phillip despairingly recorded: "No country can afford less support to the first settlers, or be more disadvantageously placed for receiving support from the mother country, on which it must for a time depend." It was a hungry year and a lonely time. "We begin to think that the mother country has entirely forsaken us", wrote a First Fleet surgeon. "...In this deplorable situation famine is staring us in the face . . . and happy is the man that can kill a rat or a crow to make him a dainty meal . . . I dined most heartily the other day on a fine dog, and I hope I shall again have an invitation to a similar repast . . ." Phillip saw that a long term answer to the problem was free settlers. There was, he wrote, a "great difference between a settlement formed such as this, and one formed by farmers and emigrants who have been used to labour and who reap the fruits of their own industry . . . Amongst the convicts we have few who are inclined to be industrious . . . upwards of one hundred . . . must ever be a burden to the settlement . . . It must, my Lord, be settlers, with the assistance of convicts, that will put this country in a situation for supporting its inhabitants . . . If settlers are sent out, many difficulties will be removed . . ."

Beautifully restored kitchen of Entally House, Hadspen, near Launceston, Tasmania. Entally House was built by Thomas Reibey, son of emancipist Mary Reibey (transported at fifteen for riding a neighbour's horse) and father of Thomas Reibey, Premier of Tasmania in 1876. Thomas Reibey retired early from his mother's commercial enterprises and built this house on a 4000 acres grant from Governor Macquarie.

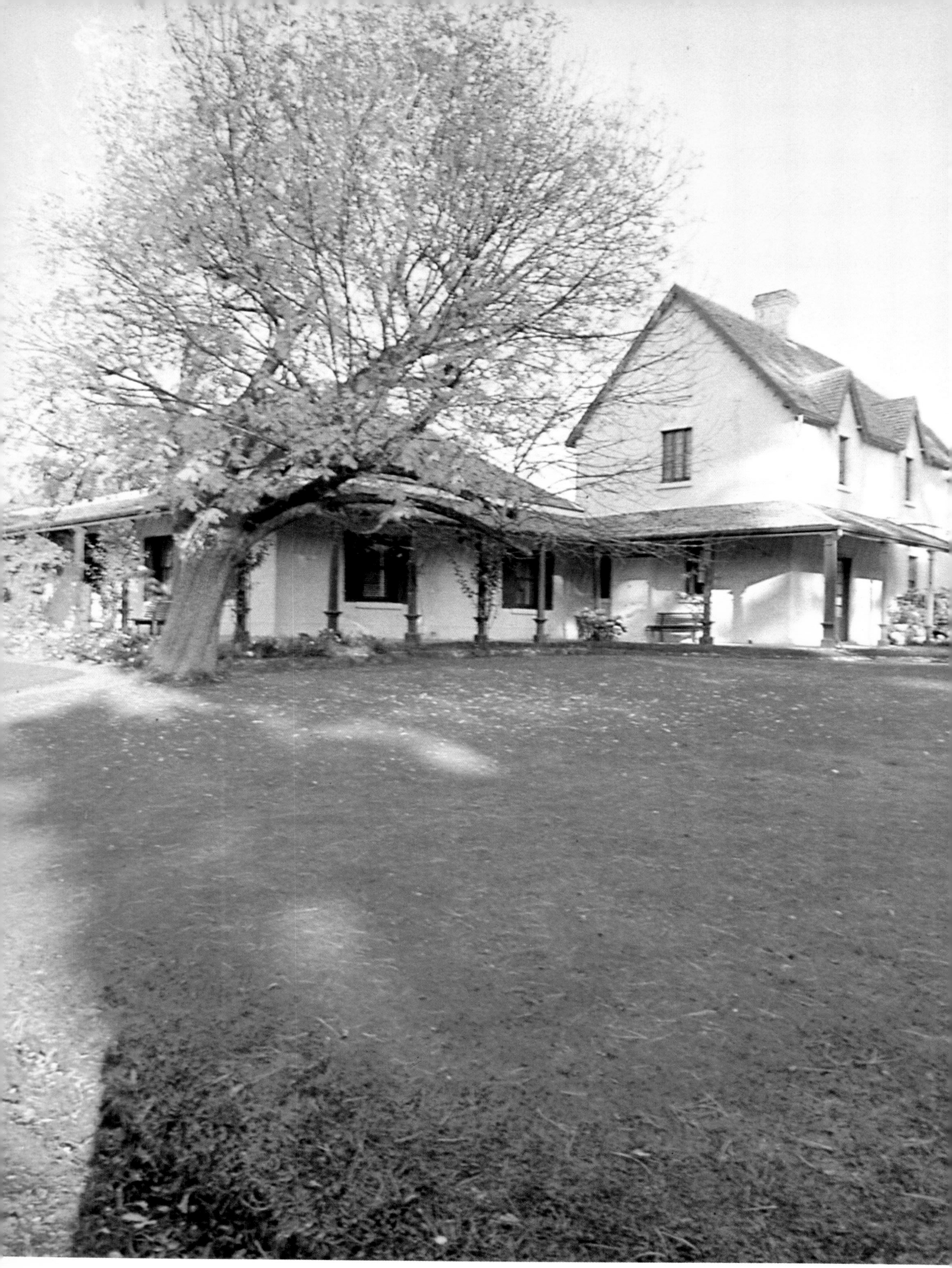

starting point...

Food, better land, and free settlers. The problem was urgent. Suitable land was found at Rose Hill, two days journey up the Parramatta River. Phillip's instructions were to grant land to those emancipated convicts and ex-soldiers who might make a success of farming. As an experiment, ex-convict James Ruse and his wife were given uncleared land at Rose Hill. Ruse diligently cleared and cultivated it and within two years declared that he was self-supporting. It was a major break-through. A trickle of settlers followed Ruse. Land was there for the asking! Hope gleaned the British Isles of those adventurous enough, enterprising enough, to try their luck in the new country. Grants were made in perpetuity to any settlers who stayed and worked their land for five years and were prepared to feed and clothe the convicts assigned as servants. Initially they were given the same concessions as Ruse: a minimum of tools and sustenance for eighteen months. The size of the grant depended upon status; unmarried emancipists (who had shown convincing signs of reformation) were on the bottom of the ladder, officers on the top; free settlers and "other ranks" were in between. Grants could also be made for special services. It was a system open to abuse.

After Phillip left the colony, this "peasant" agriculture on small holdings was destroyed by the activities of the unscrupulous N.S.W. ("Rum") Corps. These men quickly gathered power around them, ruthlessly monopolising trade and stifling the efforts of the settlers. Holdings were forced into bankruptcy and snapped up by the officers; stately manors appeared on the outskirts of Sydney. They gained a stranglehold on the wealth and resources of the colony which later Governors failed to break. Among their ranks was John Macarthur who, while the colony was still in the shadow of mass starvation, withheld his extensive holdings from the production of food and grew rich on the profits of wool farming.

Entally House, exterior. There has been a homestead on this site on the banks of the South Esk River since the early 1820's, but Entally has been much altered and added to over the years. In 1950 it was bought by the Tasmanian Government, restored and opened to the public as a period museum.

Afternoon light on an old stone farmhouse, near Swansea, Tasmania.

Wilpena Pound, early farm in the Flinders Ranges, South Australia.

Cadman's Cottage, Sydney's oldest dwelling.
Home of Sydney's first Superintendent of
Government Boats, once the waters of
Sydney Cove lapped at its front yard.

Framework of mud hut, Oberon, N.S.W. Early
settlers took their building materials from the
land around them.

Log cabin at Stony Creek, near Tumbarumba.

Cane-grass hut, Fort Grey, New South Wales.

42

This building at Bowenfels, near Lithgow, N.S.W., served as a private school in the eighteen-sixties. Some records suggest that at another stage it operated as the Royal Hotel, a way station for travellers to the farmlands and goldfields of the west.

First farm house of John Macarthur, pioneer of the Australian wool industry, at Camden, N.S.W.

Paddington pump, erected in 1869, is a relic of the district's early water supply.

A scattered group of small settlers on the rich flood flats of the Hawkesbury River struggled through these years. Their land was too distant from Sydney to be of interest to the officers, but they were defenceless in the face of the officers' trade monopoly. The settlement was harassed by Aborigines and at the mercy of the capricious flood waters of the Hawkesbury. While allowing that the soil was "uncommonly fertile" the authorities feared that "it would be the utmost imprudence to place any dependence on that settlement as a resource . . ." because of the repeated floodings. Lord Hobart, Secretary for the Colonies, suggested that the area be used for rice-growing! Yet the settlers continually returned to their sodden land, depressing and alarming Governors King and Hunter. It was Macquarie who persuaded them to move above the flood levels, founding the towns of Windsor, Richmond, Castlereagh, Pitt Town and Wilberforce on the surrounding hills. This area remains a market garden to present-day Sydney.

But the future of the country did not lie with small-time agriculture. It was the members of the Rum Corps, with their huge sheep-grazing properties, who marked the path that was to be followed by many an eager settler chasing the promise of the golden fleece onto the western plains.

44

Early settler's farm on the Derwent River, Tasmania.

Historic water well at Cape Leeuwin, Western Australia, was the sole source of fresh water for the early settlers of the 1830's. Cape Leeuwin, in the extreme south-west corner of Australia, was sighted by several of the early navigators. The area was named by the Dutch in the seventeenth century and surveyed by Flinders in 1801. First exploration by land was by Captain James Stirling in 1830. Colonisation followed soon after but made very little progress for several decades.

moving out...

Until 1805 grants were small holdings to be used for agriculture, a system which could in no way accommodate the growing wool industry. John Macarthur's grant of 5000 acres in that year changed this. The original scheme of small farms for ex-convicts was doomed and the seeds sown for the bitter quarrels between emancipists and exclusionists (officers and wealthy settlers), a battle that continued between the free selectors and the squatters. Men clamoured for land, hungrily viewing the widening horizons unveiled by the explorers. "Not a Cow calves in the colony but her owner applies for an additional grant in consequence of the encrease of his stock," lamented Governor Brisbane in 1823. "Every person to whom a grant is made receives it as the payment of a debt; every one to whom one is refused turns my implacable enemy . . ." Sale of Crown land, as opposed to free grants, began in 1824, and by 1831 the system of grants had ceased altogether. If a grazier wanted land, he had to pay; it was hoped this would curb the far-ranging land-grabbing. Land was sold at auction for a minimum price of 5/- per acre. But the flocks still needed enormous areas, land far beyond the financial reach of the graziers, who instead of bidding against each other for title, simply "squatted" on suitable Crown land. A plan to peg the settlement to definite limits "beyond which land was neither to be sold or let" was put forward in 1826 and became law in 1829. This was Governor Darling's "Nineteen Counties" — an area, considered ample for the requirements of the colony, spread in a radius of approximately 250 kilometres from Sydney, bounded in the north by the Manning River up to its source in the Mount Royal Range, west to the Wellington Valley and south to the Goulburn Plains. Beyond these boundaries ". . . settlers are not allowed to receive grants or lease land", decreed Governor Darling in 1831, while also allowing that ". . . it is impossible to prevent their sending their cattle beyond these limits . . .". Men and sheep became trespassers on Crown land; by 1830 as many were beyond the boundaries as within. As noted by Governor Bourke in 1834 ". . . In every direction the desire of procuring good pastures for sheep has led the colonists far beyond the limits of location." The Secretary of State for Colonies was indignant: "It were as unauthorised an act of presumption for an Australian squatter to drive his flocks into the recesses of the untrodden wilderness, without Her Majesty's express sanction first obtained as for a Berkshire farmer to feed his oxen, without rent or license, in the Queen's demesne of Hampton Court . . .". To these distant words from the Colonial Office Governor Bourke had a reasoned rejoinder:

47

This settler's home near Wiseman's Ferry is one of the earliest in the area.

Part of an old bullock-drawn timber jinker, Myall Lakes, N.S.W., relic of the days when great stands of cedar covered the flats of the Hunter Valley.

Old bushman and his pack-horse, Tumut area, N.S.W. The early settlers moved out across the continent in just such a way.

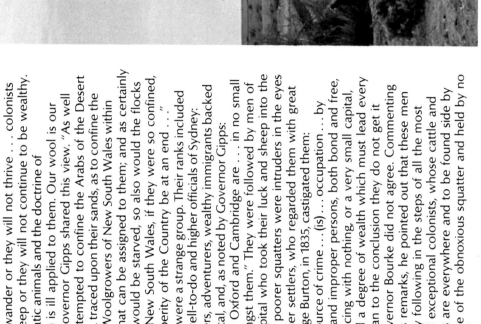

"Sheep must wander or they will not thrive . . . colonists must have sheep or they will not continue to be wealthy. Sheep are erratic animals and the doctrine of concentration is ill applied to them. Our wool is our wealth . . ." Governor Gipps shared this view. "As well might it be attempted to confine the Arabs of the Desert within a circle, traced upon their sands, as to confine the Graziers and Woolgrowers of New South Wales within any bounds that can be assigned to them; and as certainly as the Arabs would be starved, so also would the flocks and herds of New South Wales, if they were so confined, and the prosperity of the Country be at an end . . ."

The squatters were a strange group. Their ranks included many of the well-to-do and higher officials of Sydney: ex-army officers, adventurers, wealthy immigrants backed by British capital, and, as noted by Governor Gipps:

"Graduates of Oxford and Cambridge are . . . in no small number amongst them." They were followed by men of little or no capital who took their luck and sheep into the interior; these poorer squatters were intruders in the eyes of the wealthier settlers, who regarded them with great animosity. Judge Burton, in 1835, castigated them:

". . . another source of crime . . . (is) . . . occupation . . . by unauthorised and improper persons, both bond and free, who commencing with nothing, or a very small capital, soon acquired a degree of wealth which must lead every reasonable man to the conclusion they do not get it honestly." Governor Bourke did not agree. Commenting on the judge's remarks, he pointed out that these men were ". . . only following in the steps of all the most influential and exceptional colonists, whose cattle and sheep stations are everywhere and to be found side by side with those of the obnoxious squatter and held by no better title . . ."

48

Pioneer's home near Silverton, in far west of New South Wales.

Pisé hut, built of rammed mud or clay in the manner of the early settlers — near Adelaide, South Australia.

Picturesque link with early transport in Australia — Cobb and Co. inn near Kurrajong N.S.W., is still standing.

Collit's Inn, Hartley Vale, N.S.W., built by Pierce Collit who arrived in the colony as a convict in 1801. He was pardoned in 1811 and later given a grant of land. By 1823 Collit had built his inn (originally known as "The Golden Fleece"). Renowned for its service and hospitality, its doors welcomed all from governors to goldminers. Open for public inspection.

So all were squatters, but the more successful ones were men not without voice in the country. Almost all the members of the Legislative Council of 1835 were squatters, and in 1836 their position was legalised; for £10 a year they were granted licences of occupation and could take their pick of unsurveyed Crown lands outside the nominal boundaries of settlement, running as many sheep and cattle as they liked (or had) on tracts of land of any size and their own choosing. It was a simple system and for a start there was a tacit understanding that nobody would infringe on country already occupied by a squatter or take up land within a certain distance of another station. The licence gave no title, but did protect the occupancy against all intruders except the Crown; once licensed, the squatter had only to say: "I had possession before you came in." There was, of course, one great anomaly; the big stock owner with many thousands of head and vast tracts of country paid the same £10 a year as did the little man on his small holding. Both felt equally insecure. A licence lasted for one year only, and at the end of any year renewal could be refused at the whim of the Crown. Even if the squatter could afford to buy, it was not for sale. Consequently there was little inclination to spend money on property improvements or homesteads. Many of the squatters, including wealthy men controlling vast areas, ". . . whilst resident on their stations, (lived) in the most wretched way . . ."; huge holdings were managed by overseers for absentee "squatters" in Sydney and even English land companies.

Although a venture which promised high financial rewards, it was a primitive and lonely life for the men on the land. Finding a suitable run was difficult and often dangerous. Equipping the property with livestock and supplies was a lengthy and expensive business. Their shelter was often only a rough bark or slab hut, "very comfortless", with earthen floor, holes for windows and a chimney of stones and clay. Squatter and station hand together faced the isolation and dangers of pioneering in the Australian bush — the climatic whims of floods and drought, the threat of hostile Aborigines and later bushrangers. Many were forced off the land:

"Come Stumpy, old man, let's shift while we can;
Your mates in the paddock are dead . . ."
sang the broken-down squatter to his horse.

Country-town general store, Swan Hill, Vic. — blacksmith's and barber shop together.

Courthouse at Morpeth, one of the earliest towns in the Hunter Valley, N.S.W.

Old water mill in the Adelaide hills, near Hahndorf, South Australia.

Glenrock, in southern N.S.W., convict-built home of George Barber, brother-in-law of explorer Hamilton Hume, who settled in the district in the 1820's. This house saw many facets of early Australian history: southward bound exploring parties and land-seeking squatters enjoyed its hospitality.

Times and attitudes changed as the successful squatters grew wealthy and more secure:
The master was a man;
But now the squatters, puffed with pride,
They treat us with disdain . . . ;

They lamented the sheep-watcher in 1861. The first step was the battle for greater security of tenure, waged in the 1840's. Governor Gipps was strongly opposed to the sale of any land outside the "area of location" (which had by that time extended to twenty-two counties from the original nineteen). No matter what price was fixed, he argued in 1840, if it were open to the first claimant to purchase such land as he chose, ". . . a complete scramble would ensue; . . . every acre of good land would be immediately bought up by great Capitalists at whose mercy all newly arrived Emigrants would be placed . . ." and later the same year: "If unsurveyed lands are to be open to selection . . . houses . . . stockyards . . . fields which they have cultivated, the streams or pools at which they water their cattle, may henceforth be wrested from them by anyone who can run faster than they to the Land Office and there deposit a few pounds."

By 1847 the squatters had won their battle with Gipps. They were given longer leases — fourteen years in the unsettled areas and eight years in the intermediate districts — and had the option to purchase 324 acres (130 hectares) as a homestead block. This soon led to all the squatting lands being virtually locked up in the hands of less than a thousand graziers. It was, as the Land League of N.S.W. proclaimed in 1859: "practically placed as far beyond the reach of the great body of the people, as if those lands had no existence at all . . ."

But no sooner had the squatters settled in their hard-won security and the comfortable homesteads they were now prepared to build, than they felt the shudders of a growing demand to "unlock the land" for closer settlement. The squatter kings watched aghast as swarms of immigrants, fresh from the heady and lawless atmosphere of the goldfields, began to nibble at the edges of their domains. "A vote, a rifle and a farm" became the catchcry of the ex-diggers and hopeful settlers, who envisaged the rich pastures of New South Wales and Victoria divided into lots for the free selectors.

Cattle slaughterhouse, St. Marys, N.S.W., is simply constructed of timber slabs and shingles.

Crumbling remains of the mud and stone fireplace of a settler's cottage, Oberon, N.S.W.

Slab woolshed — once alive with clicking shears, blue-bellied ewes, tar boys and tall tales — Cumnock, near Bathurst, N.S.W.

Glenfield barn, Casula, N.S.W. Glenfield is a fine example of an early colonial farm house. It was built in 1817 by Charles Throsby, an early settler and explorer who arrived in Australia in 1802 as surgeon on the convict transport Coromandel. He made a number of journeys of exploration and is credited with the discovery of the site of Canberra. Throsby committed suicide at Glenfield in 1828 after a long legal battle with creditors of a friend for whom he had pledged £5000.

54

settling down....

The crunch for the squatters came with the Robertson land reform Acts of 1861; unsurveyed land could be purchased by the free selectors and the term of a squatter's lease was reduced. The bush balladists of the 1860's chortled in triumph:

There's a happy little valley by the Eumerella shore,
Where I've lingered many happy hours away,
On my little free selection I have acres by the score,
Where I unyoke the bullocks from the dray.
Oh, my pretty little calf, at the squatter you may laugh,
He will never be your owner any more,
For you're running, running, running,
on the duffer's piece of land.
Free-selected by the Eumerella shore.
To Jack Robertson we'll say, we're on a better lay,
And we'll never go a-farming any more;
For it's easier duffing cattle on the little piece of land,
Free-selected by the Eumerella shore.

The squatters responded by "dummying" (selecting land in other's names) and "peacocking" (buying up key land and waterholes). In Victoria the land reform Acts of the 1860's had loopholes large enough for the squatters to drive flocks of sheep through. They had to be tighter but further attempts at reform were blocked by the landed gentlemen of the Legislative Council, which was elected on a property franchise. Radical politician and occasional premier, Graham Berry, thunderingly denounced the pro-squatter Council as "a chamber which robs the people of ... the land God gave them ..." As Premier he succeeded in forcing through legislation which reduced the Council's power and released large areas of land to settler/farmers. Whereupon Member of the Legislative Council William Campbell decided to "retire to the old world, where communism is not so rank as it is here ..." The mighty pastoral kingdoms were crumbling, and Australia's settlement entered a new phase.

Historic oast house near Richmond, Tasmania, a great circular hop barn now converted to a most interesting house.

Riversdale, Goulburn, N.S.W., was built as an inn in the 1830's, near the junction of the Mulwaree and Wollondilly rivers. Riversdale is famous for the beauty of its woodwork; it has now been restored to its original state as an inn by the National Trust and is open for public inspection.

Dalwood in the Hunter Valley, N.S.W., where George Wyndham, winemaker and horsebreeder, planted the first vines in the 1820's.

Farm house of an early settler at Webbs Creek, near Wiseman's Ferry, N.S.W.

Stock yards of Cattle King Sir Sidney Kidman in outback Queensland show painstaking workmanship using only bush timber and hand tools. Kidman started in the 1880's as a horse and cattle trader; he bought Owen Springs Station (southwest of Alice Springs) and by 1920 had expanded his empire to cover over a hundred thousand square miles of central Australia embracing four States. He survived three severe droughts and the Depression.

The big bell at Dabee, Rylstone, N.S.W., called hands to food and toil, warned of bushfires and told of christenings. Dabee was built by Edward Cox, a brother of George and Henry Cox who discovered and pioneered the Mudgee district, and a son of William Cox who built the road over the Blue Mountains. Dabee, now a National Trust house, is noted for its outstanding woolshed.

Homestead at Wantabadgery, N.S.W. Charles Sturt was in the area in 1829 (he called it "Pontebadgery"). The homestead was held up by bushrangers in 1878.

Early settler's home at Albany, W.A. First white settlement in Western Australia was established at King George's Sound in 1826 to prevent possible French colonisation and to claim the whole continent as a British possession. Originally called Frederickstown, after Frederick, Duke of York and Albany, brother of George III and heir to the throne, the name was quickly dropped in favour of Albany. At first the settlement was administered by New South Wales, but after the establishment of a colony at Swan River (Perth) in 1831, control was transferred there.

Historic home of Marshall Clifton at Australind, near Bunbury, W.A., scene of an ambitious colonisation scheme proposed in 1839 by the Western Australian Company. A splendid town plan was drawn up in London along the lines of an English country centre, with market square, churches, town hall and other public buildings. The surrounding country was divided into 100 acre farm allotments and offered for sale to prospective settlers at £1 per acre. Proceeds were to provide free passage for farm labourers — convicts were excluded from Western Australia at the time and great difficulty had been experienced in obtaining workers. When the first group of settlers arrived, led by Marshall Clifton, Commissioner, the town was already laid out and the farms surveyed, but all were still virgin bush. The emigrant labourers they hoped would clear and cultivate them preferred to go to the eastern colonies. The settlers, who had expected to live in town and have their farms worked by hired hands, found they had to do their own work or starve. As the land, in any case, proved unsuitable for intensive cultivation, they soon followed their labourers in the drift to find better conditions elsewhere. Within three years the settlement was virtually abandoned, though Marshall Clifton and his large family stayed on, eventually after much hardship acquiring a degree of comfort.

Interior of St Malo, Hunters Hill, N.S.W. Built in 1847, it was the home of Didier Joubert, who bought 200 acres from Mary Reibey at Fig Tree when the only access to the area was by rowing boat. He established the first ferry service to Hunters Hill, built many of the beautiful homes that still stand there, was responsible for the erection of bridges over Iron Cove and the Parramatta River at Gladesville, and was Mayor of Hunters Hill, 1867-9, after it became one of Sydney's earliest municipalities. Despite a desperate effort to save it, this fine home was demolished recently to make way for an expressway. The resultant outcry was so great that it could probably be said that the sacrifice of St Malo saved many other historic homes from destruction.

growth...

A century after the First Fleeters waded ashore to the chilling silence of the Port Jackson bush, Australia had settled into an energetic yet ordered way of life. Merchants, traders and shopkeepers handled the rich produce of the squatters and farmers; the settlement lost the makeshift frontier look and grew to cities whose streets were lined with solid stone buildings — testimony to the country's prosperity. The challenge of the land had been met and as wealth was gained from the soil so there grew a rich and influential mercantile class, middle men who supplied both the squatters and retail stores with imported and other goods.

The first "trade monopoly" was held by the Government Store. All cargoes which came into the country were the King's, and such produce as the settlers wrung from the soil they had to sell to the King at fixed prices. King George III was the colony's first storekeeper! All the necessaries of life were rationed from his Store, without payment in the early years. In the turmoil of the three years following the departure of Governor Phillip and the arrival of Hunter, a group of officers from the N.S.W. Corps usurped this monopoly from the Crown, gaining exclusive rights to all cargoes which they then retailed at handsome profits or wholesaled to emancipated convicts acting as dealers. Their monopoly extended over the farm goods of the colony — settlers were forced to make unprofitable sales as producers and to pay exhorbitant prices as consumers. The "Rum Corps", as the group was known, prospered; the farmer struggled. "Many of the inferior farmers were nearly ruined by the high price that they were obliged to give for such necessaries as they required from those who had long been in the habit of monopolising every article brought to the settlement for sale, a habit of which it was found impossible to get the better . . ." (wrote Judge Advocate Collins). Mrs John Macarthur viewed the activities of her husband and his fellow officers from another angle. She wrote to a friend: "The officers in the colony, with a few others possessed of money and credit in England, unite together and purchase the cargoes of such vessels as repair to this country from various quarters. Two or more are chosen from the number to bargain for the cargo offered for sale, which is then divided amongst them in proportion to the amount of their subscriptions . . . These details which may seem prolix are necessary to show you the mode in which we are in our infant condition compelled to proceed . . ."

61

Sweeping staircase of Manar, near Goulburn, N.S.W. Hugh Gordon built this house (c. 1840) for his bride, Mary King Macarthur, daughter of Hannibal Macarthur, niece of Phillip Parker King and granddaughter of Governor King. It was named for his Scottish estate at Invercurie, Aberdeenshire, and the garden was planted with seeds brought from Scotland.

Bells at Horsley, Smithfield, N.S.W., used for summoning servants.

Newington, Silverwater, N.S.W. This fine mansion was built in 1832. It features a verandah supported by Doric columns — the shaft of each column is carved from a single piece of stone. Designer is unknown.

Legacy of the German pioneer settlers in South Australia — Lutheran Church at Tanunda in the Barossa Valley, S.A.

Governors Hunter, King, Bligh and Macquarie battled to break this monopoly; one way was to encourage the growth of an independent merchant body in the colony. The first of such was a Scot, Robert Campbell, merchant and shipowner who had earlier been forced to sell his imports to the military. He purchased land on the eastern shore of Sydney Cove for his wharves, and after obtaining the readily forthcoming permission from Governor King, Campbell and Company went into business. By 1804 the growing firm had £50,000 worth of goods in its Sydney warehouses. Campbell was greatly admired for his honest trading, and his action in competing with the officers was appreciated. Two hundred grateful settlers provided him with a memorial which read: "But for you, we had still been prey to the Mercenary unsparing Hand of Avarice and Extortion." Campbell's enterprise opened the way for other merchants.

Prominent in the ranks of these early merchants were emancipists. Simeon Lord, sentenced to seven years' transportation for stealing "100 yards of muslin valued at sixpence and 100 yards of calico valued at fourpence," arrived in Sydney in 1791. By 1798 he was employing labour and quickly established himself as a leading commercial figure. A shipowner and storekeeper, with interests extending to the South Sea Islands, he grew rich on the trading profits of coal, sealskin, whale oil, sheepskins, timber and wheat. Lord also attempted manufacture — he had a contract to "burl, mill, dress and dye" cloth from the Parramatta factory, made hats and glassware and later established a woollen mill — but his enterprise in this direction was frowned upon by Commissioner Bigge who felt that local manufacture would rob England of export markets. Lord was highly regarded by the settlers as a fair trader; he was known to supply goods and also money to those down on their luck, receiving payment "as it suited their convenience at a distant period and without interest". He was prominent in the feuds between Emancipists and Exclusionists which broke out during Macquarie's governorship. John Macarthur, erstwhile member of the Rum Corps that had held the colony to ransom, was livid when, while exiled in England for his part in the Rum Rebellion, he heard of the Governor's association with Lord and other leading emancipists. "Would to God I could withdraw you from the colony . . ." he wrote to his wife. "Is it possible . . . that Governor Macquarie can . . . bring to his table men who have been convicts — who have amassed fortunes by the most infamous frauds . . .?"

65

Old Overland Telegraph Station — original site of Alice Springs — near one of the few semi-permanent water holes on the Todd River, central Australia. The stations of the Overland Telegraph were spread across the continent and were often used as bases by explorers in the early 1870's. This station was the first settlement in the Alice Springs area. Settlers took up land in the late 1870's and a township called Stuart grew two miles downstream; the name, Alice Springs, originally given to the station, was soon adopted for the new settlement. The Telegraph Station, the water hole, and 400 hectares of land surrounding it, are now a National Park. Most of the old buildings on the site have been restored to their original condition.

Townsville Hotel, Townsville, Queensland, is a fine example of the delicate "iron lace" featured in much of Australia's architecture last century.

Convict-built, this bridge across the Coal River at Richmond, Tasmania, is the oldest still existing in Australia. The six-arched bridge was designed by Major Bell of the 48th Regiment and was completed in 1825. The township of Richmond, just north of Hobart, is one of the earliest settled districts in Tasmania. The area was explored in 1803 by Lt. John Bowen, who discovered small deposits of coal there (hence the name "Coal River").

Female Orphan School, Parramatta, N.S.W. In 1801 Governor King commenced building an orphanage on this site but the work was later abandoned after a few makeshift buildings had been erected. Work was restarted in 1813 at the direction of Governor Macquarie — with Samuel Marsden in charge of construction — but dragged on year after year and was not completed until 1818. First known as the Protestant Orphanage, it catered for both boys and girls, but in 1842 was restricted to girls only. The school became part of a mental hospital in 1888, a capacity in which it still serves. There have been several additions and alterations to the original "Colonial barrack" architecture of the building. The porch is a modern addition and the graceful wings of the original design have been masked and altered.

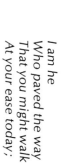

Builders

The men and women who built Australia were a fascinating cross section of the English community carted halfway across the world and tumbled together in a puzzling and hostile land where even the stars were strange. The keystone of Australia's foundation was the transportation system — in no other way could such a diverse collection of humanity be gathered together in such an unlikely place. It mattered little if they came as convict or corporal, all were exiles, banished from England and everything that was familiar and bound to each other by the common need for survival.

The convicts themselves were a motley lot. In their ranks were to be found political rebels — Irish patriots and trade unionists from Tolpuddle — humble men of the soil or slums exiled for minor crimes, and rogues of gentle birth who had also fallen foul of the system. They were guarded by men fearful for their existence in this colony of felons, who carried out their duties with satanic savagery; by men of vision who believed that the colony could grow past a gaol. To these were added the early free settlers, men hungry for land, families seeking to swop desperate destitution in crowded slums for the chance to make their own way in the loneliness of the new land. From all these came the nation builders.

banished...

The convict, James Ruse, was perhaps the first of the strangely assorted group of exiles to come to grips with the task of building a new homeland. Ruse, a "Natef of Cornwell" transported with the First Fleet in 1788, had already spent five of his seven years' sentence on the hulks at Plymouth. When his term expired in 1789 he was installed by Governor Phillip on two acres of land at Rose Hill (Parramatta) as an experiment "... in order to know in what time a man might be able to cultivate a sufficient quantity of ground to support himself." Ruse was given farming tools, seed and some livestock, and told that if he could maintain himself he would be given thirty acres of land as a grant. Ruse, who described himself as "bred a husbandman", set about preparing his land carefully, burning off fallen timber, digging in the ashes and then the grass and weeds that followed so that, as he put it, "it was not like the Government farm, just scratched over, but properly done ... I let it lie as long as I, could, exposed to air and sun ... My straw, I mean to bury in pits, and throw in with it everything which I think will rot and turn to manure ..." The crops throve and in 1791 Ruse reported himself able to maintain his family from its produce. The promised grant of thirty acres was duly made — the first land grant in New South Wales, number one on the official register.

On his tombstone, Ruse is claimed to have "sowd the forst Grain" and some quibble about this, claiming the seed he sowed at Experiment Farm was actually from the first harvest gathered in the colony at the Government farm. Ruse himself acknowledged this: "On my wheat land I sowed three bushels of seed, the produce of this country, broadcast," he reported to Captain Watkin Tench in 1790. However, he was certainly the first to have become self-sufficient from the land, and as he had been chosen for the "experiment" because he had proved himself capable and industrious, may well have commended himself to Governor Phillip by work on the Government farm itself, and sowed his first seed there! He was possibly the only one among a collection of pickpockets and starving city slum dwellers who had ever held a shovel in his hands before; the great bulk of the convicts came from London, its suburbs and the principal cities.

Lennox Bridge, on Lapstone Hill in the Blue Mountains of N.S.W., is the oldest on the mainland of Australia. A single-arched stone bridge across a small steep gully, it was designed and supervised by David Lennox, Scottish stonemason and the colony's first capable bridge-builder, who emigrated in 1832 in middle age; the bridge, his first, was completed the following year. Although by-passed by the Great Western Highway, it was still used by vehicular traffic until very recently. Lennox also designed the Landsdowne Bridge over Prospect Creek at Liverpool, N.S.W. (completed 1836). This is still in use by Sydney-bound traffic on the Hume Highway.

71

Tombstone of James Ruse, in the churchyard of St. John's, Campbelltown, N.S.W. The inscription on his tombstone reads:

My Mother reread Me Tenderly
With Me She Took Much Paines
And When I Arived In This Coelney
I sowd the Forst Grain And Now
With My Hevenly Father I Hope
For Ever To Remain

Elizabeth Farmhouse, Parramatta, N.S.W. The oldest existing house in Australia, it was built in 1793 by John Macarthur (who probably acted as his own architect) on his first land grant in 1793. Named for his wife Elizabeth it was home to the Macarthur family for nearly forty years and centre of the famous Macarthur flocks. The house is regarded as the prototype of Australian colonial architecture — the roof sweeps down, extending past the walls to surround the house with cool verandahs.

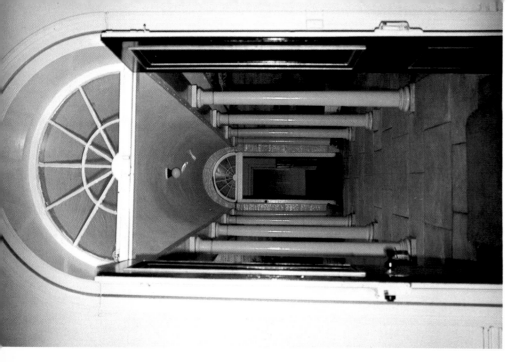

Colourful and aristocratic Sir Henry Brown Hayes, transported in 1801 for abducting a young Quaker heiress, was the original owner of Vaucluse, near the South Head of Port Jackson. Sir Henry did not behave like a convict. He paid the master of the transport that brought him to New South Wales a large sum of money to obtain special favours, and monopolised most of the free space and available comforts, much to the annoyance of the free settlers and officials who were travelling on the same vessel. Within six months of arrival he was given a ticket of leave and within twelve months had bought himself the property beside the harbour which he called Vaucluse. He built the original Vaucluse House in 1803 and (to keep the snakes at bay!) surrounded his estate with a strip of genuine Irish peat specially imported from Ireland and dug into place by convicts of Irish birth. After Hayes, Vaucluse was owned briefly by Captain John Piper, who sold it to William Charles Wentworth in 1827. Wentworth set about building onto Hayes' beginnings and Vaucluse House as it now stands was completed in 1829. The unusual architecture of the house is a fanciful mixture of mediaeval Gothic (crenellated walls, turrets and battlements) and the wide surrounding verandahs of the Australian colonial style. It is now a State Historic Site, restored as a museum of the period and open to the public. The surrounding grounds have been retained as a park.

Robert Campbell, younger son of the last Laird of Ashfield, Argyllshire, Scotland, connected with the Campbell clan of Duntrune Castle, came to Sydney in 1798 as a shipowner and trader. He built Campbell's Wharf on the east shore of Sydney Cove and in 1825 was granted 5000 acres on the Limestone Plains (Canberra) as part compensation for the loss of a vessel which the Government had commandeered from him. He named his property Duntroon and his overseer, James Ainslie, established the district's second settlement there, probably late the same year. In 1833 Campbell commenced building Duntroon House, the stone homestead which today, with various additions over the years, forms part of the Royal Military College.

...rior doorway at Vaucluse House,
...cluse, N.S.W. This early colonial mansion,
...once the home of pioneer statesman
...am Charles Wentworth.

...ee House, on Lane Cove River, N.S.W.,
...ed once by emancipist-merchant Mary
...ey and then by the ferrymaster, Hunters
...oioneer Didier Joubert. Didier extended
...house by adding first a timber room,
...ed to fit the roots of the massive
...eton Bay figtree from which the area got
...ame, and then a two storey stone
...nsion. His son, Numa Joubert, added the
...er tower much later.

...nificent curved stairway of Elizabeth Bay
...se, Elizabeth Bay, N.S.W. Designed by
... Verge, it was built in 1832 for Alexander
...leay, Colonial Secretary and
...nguished botanist. Its grounds once
...ered more than fifty acres and were
...ded with splendid native and exotic
...bs and trees.

...roon House, Canberra, A.C.T.

Australia's early defences were the results of threats which never eventuated. Ripples from the waves of war and political crises in another hemisphere, they followed vaguely the course of events in the world left behind. Revolution broke out in France; a battery of guns was mounted on the western shore of Sydney Cove, Australia (by Lt Dawes, on the point which now bears his name). Napoleon thundered across Europe, and an emplacement sprang up on Georges Head, commanding the harbour entrance. Greenway, the convict architect, conceived a detailed plan for the defence of the entire Sydney region but it was never fully carried out. His design for Fort Macquarie (on Bennelong Point, site of the Opera House) was completed in 1821 but his grandiose scheme for a citadel on Observatory Hill, with the Dawes Point battery as an outwork, was vetoed by Commissioner Bigge and never finished. Early one morning in 1839 Sydney residents awoke to find two American warships nonchalantly swinging at anchor. They had slipped, unaided and unnoticed, into the harbour during the night. This aroused considerable alarm and led to renewed interest in strengthening the defences of the town. Work was begun on Pinchgut (Fort Denison). To the outrage of eminent citizen Dr John Dunmore Lang, the pinnacle of rock on the island was levelled and the ground was prepared for building (he described it as an act of "Goths and vandals" to remove the rocky peak and replace it with a "gingerbread fortification"). A shortage of funds caused the project to be abandoned until ripples from the Crimean War aroused fears of a "Russian threat". Once again the military looked to the island. Work was restarted and the fort, with its Martello tower and stone walls twelve feet thick, was completed in 1857

Victoria Barracks, Sydney, N.S.W., were built on the sandy windswept hills of Paddington. Construction was begun in 1841, to the plans of Major George Barney, and they were occupied in 1848, replacing the dilapidated Wynyard Barracks. A graceful complex of sandstone buildings, recognised as one of the finest examples of nineteenth century British Military architecture, they are probably the largest group of buildings remaining erected by convict labour.

Lancer Barracks, Parramatta, N.S.W., is the oldest continually used military barracks on mainland Australia. Building started in 1818 on the orders of Governor Macquarie; style is Georgian, walls are of sandstock brick and the designer was Lt.John Watts of the 46th Regiment. Still standing are the two storey main building and single storey officers' quarters (Bobs Hall). They served as barracks for men of British regiments, some of whom would have served in the Napoleonic wars.

75

Barracks at Garden Island, Sydney, N.S.W. In the early days of the first settlement at Sydney Cove, Garden Island was used as a source of farm produce for the *Sirius*, *Supply*, and *Lady Nelson*; later it was a convalescent and quarantine station and finally a naval depot. In 1883 it was chosen as the naval headquarters for New South Wales. The barracks, designed by James Barnett, were completed in 1887.

Fort Denison, Sydney Harbour, was first used as a dump for troublesome convicts, who were marooned there on short rations — hence the colloquial name, "Pinchgut", which persists to this day.

Bare Island, off La Perouse, Botany Bay, N.S.W. A defence battery was built there in the 1880's but was in full use for only ten years. Now a declared Historic Site.

traders...

Whaling vessels were in full-scale operation in the waters off the east coast of Australia almost before the first successful crop had been wrung from the soil at Rose Hill. Indeed the first whaler, a British ship, *Emilia*, arrived in 1788 in the wake of the First Fleet. Whaling and sealing was a highly profitable and cut-throat business. Early whalers found the creatures in profusion (they were so thick in the Derwent that boats had to be kept inshore to avoid collisions) and the cry, "Thar' she blows!" rang out from many a coastal lookout. Greedy and shortsighted harvesting soon reduced their numbers and the surviving whales moved farther out to sea — away from the strange new menace. The industry was more than a simple battle between men and waves and whales — it was marked by savage friction between rival concerns. Prior to 1813 independent British whalers were restricted in their activities by the British East India Co. which had a monopoly over British trade in the Indian and Pacific Oceans. The Americans, however, could act as free agents and soon had control of the industry despite attempts by the colony's Governors to discourage them. By the 1830's the industry was booming. By the 1840's Hobart was the greatest whaling port in the British Empire, if not the world, and up to sixty whale boats crowded into the Derwent at the same time. By the mid 1850's the industry was on the decline and by the time of the American Civil War (1861-66) most of the Americans had withdrawn. Benjamin Boyd was a British financier and adventurer who came to the colony in the 1840's. His seven year stay was marked by the growth and collapse of a huge and ambitious commercial enterprise encompassing whaling, cattle-trading, shipping, banking and politics, of which whaling is perhaps the best remembered. He dreamed of developing Twofold Bay into a major world trading centre and established Boydtown there, with wharves, stores, hotel, church, salting and boiling down works, cottages for his employees and the lighthouse and whaling lookout tower which still stands on the hill above, with his name carved deep into the stone of the turret. All the bricks used in the construction of the township had to be transported from Sydney. In 1848 Boyd had nine whalers working from the bay and the catch for the year was worth £42,000; but when failure of his banking interests reduced him to bankruptcy the following year the project collapsed and was reclaimed by the bush. Boyd left to seek his fortune on the Californian goldfields and disappeared in the Solomon Islands on the return trip in 1851. His ship *Wanderer*, continued to Australia and an expedition sent in search of him returned with a skull believed at the time to be Benjamin Boyd's. It is now considered to be that of a female Melanesian.

77

Interior of the lighthouse and whaling lookout tower at Twofold Bay, N.S.W.

Boyd's "Sea Horse Inn", Twofold Bay.

Convict-built wall, remnant of Australia's first whaling station, on Peggy Point, Bicheno, Tasmania. From the 1800's until the 1840's whaling was Australia's most successful industry and Tasmania was one of the most important whaling centres in the world.

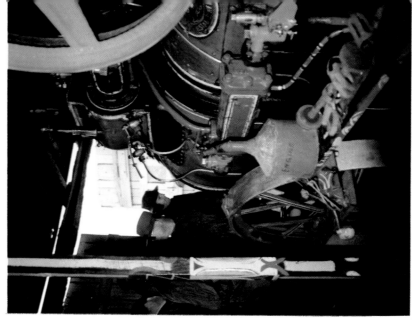

tillers...

It was a soldier, John Macarthur, officer of the N.S.W. Corps, who set the colony in the direction of a wealthy primary-producing nation. Macarthur arrived with his wife Elizabeth in 1790 aboard the *Scarborough* — a pugnacious and dynamic character who was to dominate the colonial scene for three decades. He openly boasted that he had played a part in the removal from office of every governor from Hunter to Macquarie, severely wounded his commanding officer in a duel, was in almost perpetual conflict with practically everyone with whom he came in contact, and was officially "pronounced a lunatic" in 1832. But his experiments with sheepbreeding and his work in establishing Australia's wool industry place him in the foremost ranks of the men who made Australia.

Macarthur envisaged the development of the colony in terms of a wealthy landed gentry served by convict labour. He received a grant of land at Parramatta, built Elizabeth Farm House there, imported the colony's first iron plough, and by the end of 1794 was the colony's most substantial farmer and stockholder. In conjunction with the Reverend Samuel Marsden and convict Isaac Nichols he experimented with sheep-breeding, crossing long-haired Bengal and Irish breeds, looking for wool rather than mutton. Sent to England in 1801 following his duel with Colonel Paterson, he made use of his enforced stay to promote his plans for wool. Samples of his fleece so impressed Colonial Secretary Lord Camden that he persuaded the British Government to allow Macarthur to resign his commission (thus avoiding court martial) and approve his return to the colony as a private citizen. So Macarthur returned triumphant to Sydney, bringing with him Spanish merino sheep selected from the flocks of King George III at Kew and bearing a letter ordering Governor King to grant him 5000 acres of land of his own choosing. He chose Cowpastures, to the fury of Governor King who had planned to establish a Government cattle-breeding project there, and named his selection Camden Park. He knew that he had turned the mercantile eyes of England towards Australia as a source of raw material — wool — and set about the breeding of wool sheep in earnest.

Others were moving along the same lines. Grazing properties sprang up on the outskirts of the settlement and flocks soon spread over all available land east of the Blue Mountains. Sheep were the driving force that broke the mountain barriers and opened up the vast grazing lands of the western plains and to the south. They herded the explorers before them, and those anonymous men who stealthily staked out their runs in lands still unseen by the explorers. Australia had entered the pastoral age.

Cattle sale in progress in front of the historic
Oatland Mill, Tasmania (1832).

Early technology of the Australian wool
industry — steam engine in the woolshed of
Kurrajong Park, near Cassillis, N.S.W.

Steam engine for wool-scouring, Mount
Woods Station, N.S.W.

Blacksmith's bellows, Kurrajong Park, N.S.W.

Huge wool press, Kinchega, N.S.W.

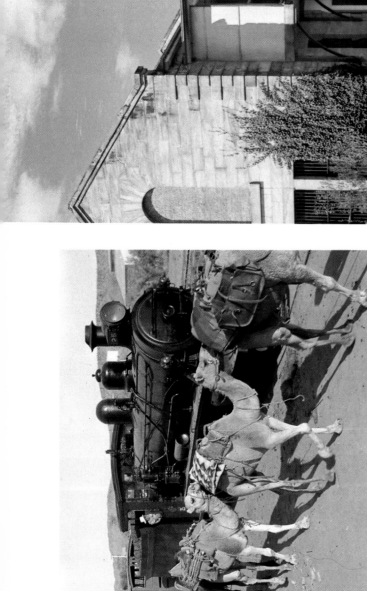

Transport in the developing country ranged from windjammer to paddlewheel steamer, from bullock waggon to camel train. Changing patterns changed fortunes. In the early days of the colony Morpeth was the hub of the Hunter, the port to which all the wool and wine, wheat and cedar, was carried by bullock-drawn waggons. The wharves by the river banks were a forest of masts and great sailing ships passed in orderly procession over reaches that today a rowboat could scarcely negotiate. The silting of the river, the railway to Newcastle, the bypassing of Morpeth by the main road highways, all combined to topple the town from its position as a great port and today it is a charming backwater of history where old stone buildings and disused wharves drowse in the sun, dreaming of the past. In the Centre, Afghans and their camels played a notable part in exploration and development. They conveyed explorers and surveyors, conducted postal services and transported supplies to settlers. When rail replaced the camels on the route between Adelaide and Alice Springs, the mixed goods and passenger train was given the affectionate name of "The Ghan" — a corruption of Afghan Express — harking back to the days when the only transport was by camel teams.

The first paddlesteamers were used on the coastal trade, shipping coal from the mines around Newcastle and plying between Port Jackson and the settlements at Port Phillip and Van Diemen's Land. With the opening up of the interior and the settlement of South Australia they moved onto the inland rivers, transporting wool and other produce to markets and carrying provisions to settlers along the Murray and Darling and goldminers on the Goulburn. When a colony was established in South Australia high hopes were held of a vast volume of traffic coming down the Murray to a major outlet at the river's mouth. But nothing eventuated, and in 1850 the South Australian Government offered a prize of £2000 for each of the first two steamers to navigate the Murray from the river's mouth to its junction with the Darling. This challenge was not taken up for two years and when it was, the first two vessels to travel up the Murray waged a

Camel team passes the old "Ghan" train, Alice Springs, N.T.

The old stone bond stores at Morpeth, N.S.W., built in 1850.

The old Woolwich Dock, Sydney, N.S.W. Excavated into the natural sandstone this large dry dock was begun by Mort's Dock Co. in 1898.

Paddlewheel steamer on the Murray River, near Mildura, Victoria. Of the many inland rivers of Australia only two, the Darling and the Murray, are navigable by large vessels. The paddle steamers which braved the hazards of sunken logs and sandbars were responsible for opening up large areas of the upper Darling district and the birth of many towns along the banks of both rivers.

Old railway engines at Zeehan, Tasmania, a reminder of earlier days when Zeehan was a prosperous mining town and known as the "Silver City of the South". The town takes its name from the nearby mountain named in 1642 by Abel Tasman after his ship Zeehaen. Zeehan came into being in 1898 following the discovery of rich silver and lead deposits in the area and at the turn of the century was a bustling community, fourth largest in Tasmania. After the failure of the mines in 1908 Zeehan saw years of decline and is now almost a ghost town.

The Central Australian Railway and the Overland telegraph line march side by side across country made green by rare seasonal rains, bringing news and supplies to the inhabitants of the Centre.

A disused train carriage stands beside eucalypt near Alice Springs, N.T.

Sydney's first steam tram now operates at Parramatta Park, N.S.W., bringing a touch of travel in the past to visitors. Sydney's first tramway, opened in 1861, ran along Pitt Street between Circular Quay and Redfern Station. It was horse-drawn and the subject of much controversy as the rails (which had to be laid upside down to fit the wheels) projected well above street level making carriage travel in Pitt Street very uncomfortable. As a result Pitt Street was avoided by the carriage trade to the dismay of the local shopkeepers. The line was closed in 1866 and the rails removed. In 1876 the steam tramway was opened and by 1898, when electrification began, there were nearly forty miles of rails and over a hundred steam engines in use.

dramatic race. One was the *Mary Ann*, built by William Randell, a flour miller of Gumeracha who knew nothing of boat building or the Government's bounty but was seized by the possibilities of a trading steamer on the Murray River. The other was the *Lady Augusta*, skippered by Francis Cadell, a shipbuilder who managed to up the Government's offer to include a bonus of £500 if he could take a steam vessel through the Murray mouth, £1000 if he could reach the junction with the Darling, and a further £1000 if he kept his vessel running on the river for twelve months. The *Mary Ann* was the first on the river. Built of red gum on the banks of the Murray, she was launched at Mannum in March, 1853, but was stopped by a sandbar after travelling little over a hundred miles as the river had fallen below normal levels due to drought. They set off again in August of the same year, when there was plenty of water in the river, but by this time Cadell had completed the *Lady Augusta* and brought her successfully through the Murray mouth to Goolwa with a party of V.I.P.'s including the Governor on board. He overtook Randell near the junction with the Murrumbidgee, well past the Darling. Randell had the *Mary Ann* tied up to the river bank there and was startled by an unusual noise on the water and the sight of the *Lady Augusta* steaming up the river and past him. Randell promptly set off after her and the two vessels raced each other to Swan Hill, the *Lady Augusta*, the more powerful steamer, winning by a few hours. There Randell took the lead again and went on to Moama, far past the *Lady Augusta*'s highest point. Neither skipper collected the original reward offered (apparently the steamers did not satisfy the Government's stipulations) but Cadell collected the £2500 for which he had negotiated and Randell a special grant of £600 plus £450 from public subscriptions. Both continued to operate steamers on the Murray for some years.

Old winery at Chateau Tahbilk, Tabilk, Victoria, built in 1860 and first worked by a Frenchman, Ludovic Marie, from Burgundy. First vines in Australia were planted by John Macarthur at Camden in 1820, followed by James Busby and George Wyndham in the Hunter Valley in the 1830's.

Wagga Wagga Court House, N.S.W., was the first public building in Wagga, being established in 1847. The town itself was not marked out until 1849 (by Surveyor Townsend) and by that time, in addition to the courthouse, boasted an inn, a store and private dwellings. The land around had been settled in the 1830's in the wake of Charles Sturt and his exploring party.

St John's Church, Canberra, A.C.T., is surrounded by graves of pioneer settlers.

Church at Bodalla, N.S.W., built 1885. Merchant Thomas Sutcliffe Mort had always wanted to build a church at Bodalla but died in 1878 before this was realised and the granite and limestone church was erected by his family as a memorial to him. It was designed by Edmund Blacket, a close friend to whom Mort's death was a great grief.

Interior of St John's Church, Bega, N.S.W. Designed by Edmund Blacket and completed in 1878 it is considered to be one of Blacket's finest country churches.

administrators...

The first administrators were English imports, naval and military men who ruled and regimented, fearful that their absolute authority might be breached in this garrisoned colony of convicts and their restless guards. Slowly there came whisperings from a new breed — free settlers and Australian born, who resented the autocratic rule and determined to have a part in their country's future.

When William Charles Wentworth was appointed acting Provost-Marshal in 1811 he became, at the age of twenty-one, the first native-born Australian to hold an important official position. It proved to be but the first step in a lifetime devoted to the service of the new colony. For more than half a century Wentworth was intimately involved in all facets of colonial politics. He fought tirelessly and successfully for representative and responsible government in Australia. He championed the cause of the emancipists (former convicts who had been pardoned) and supported the humanist policies of Macquarie in this regard. He defended freedom of the press and his outspoken newspaper, the *Australian*,

renjoey Lighthouse, Broken Bay, N.S.W., d the grave of its first keeper, George ulhall, who was killed by lightning while thering firewood during a storm. This ndstone lighthouse, designed by Colonial chitect Barnett, is one of only two along e Australian coast not painted white. Four uses, also of natural stone, were erected the staff. It was completed in 1881.

ourt House, Windsor, N.S.W. Built in 1819 to e design of Francis Greenway and still in e, this simple colonial brick courthouse is e of the few Greenway buildings to main unspoilt. Unlike other Greenway ildings such as the Supreme Court, Sydney, ich suffered at the hands of later chitects until the simple lines of the iginal were obliterated, it has happily aped attention over the years. In recent eful restoration work each brick was ersed to show a fresh face.

91

Victoria's first Government House, now transferred from its original site to the Botanic Gardens, Melbourne, Vic. La Trobe, appointed Superintendent of Port Phillip in 1839 and later its first Governor after separation from New South Wales, brought the prefabricated house with him in sections when he came out from England and it was his home when he took over as Governor. The simple wooden house now stands among eucalypts on the edge of the gardens he founded.

Old Government House, Parramatta, N.S.W. This, the oldest public building in Australia, was completed in 1816 to the design of Lt. John Watts, aided by convict-architect Francis Greenway. It incorporates two earlier structures on the site. A small lath and plaster cottage was built for Phillip shortly after the establishment of the colony; by the time of Governor Hunter's arrival in 1799 it had fallen into disrepair, but traces remain under the floorboards of the present house. Hunter ordered the construction of a new building — a two storeyed Georgian house of brick, with joinery of unpainted local cedar, and this remains as the front section of the central block. Macquarie's additions were a two storeyed building joined to the back of Hunter's structure, a portico (Greenway's) and two wings joined to the main block by a colonnade. All early governors up to the time of Fitzroy used Parramatta Government House.

Tomb of explorer-statesman William Charles Wentworth at Vaucluse House, Sydney, N.S.W. Wentworth, a "currency lad" born on Norfolk Island in 1790, was the first Australian-born to hold an important official position in the colony. Popularly remembered for his part in the crossing of the Blue Mountains with Blaxland and Lawson in 1813, his most important contributions to the young colony were made in the political arena.

published without government permission, established the precedent that was to ensure that freedom in the colony... Yet he was a man of strange contradictions. He vigorously campaigned against the cessation of transportation and envisaged an Upper House based on a colonial hereditary peerage. He played an important role in the founding of Sydney University but denounced Sir Henry Parkes, champion of compulsory free education, as an "arch anarchist". In his later life he declared: "I deny emphatically that I was ever a democrat or a republican I shall die with conservative principles".

William Charles Wentworth, the "currency lad", was born on Norfolk Island in 1790. His father was D'Arcy Wentworth, scion of a noble family, twice tried for highway robbery but never convicted (though it was said that the charges were dropped on condition that he came to Botany Bay of his own volition.) His mother was a convict girl from Staffordshire, transported for stealing "wearing apparell", with whom D'Arcy Wentworth had formed an association on the journey out and who bore him three sons during his period as a surgeon on Norfolk Island. In 1796 the family returned to Sydney, and in 1803 after the death of their mother, the two elder boys were sent to England for a gentleman's education — D'Arcy Wentworth had by this time built up a large personal fortune as a landowner and businessman.

William Charles returned to the land of his birth at the age of twenty. Three years later he accompanied Blaxland and Lawson on their epic crossing of the Blue Mountains and for this achievement received a grant of 1000 acres from a grateful government. He added this to the 1750 acres he had been given on his appointment as Provost-Marshal, thus becoming a man of considerable property in his own right. Over the years he added to his holdings, acquiring Vaucluse House and surrounding estate in 1829, numerous other estates elsewhere and leases on squatting runs. He was always a spokesman for the landed classes and his campaign for self-government never envisaged "one man one vote"; he advocated high property qualifications for members of parliament with the right to vote exercised only by those with a stake in the country. He was no "ruffian leveller", he proclaimed; while pressing for civil rights for former convicts and their offspring, he stipulated these should apply only if they measured up to the property requirements.

Ewenton, Balmain, N.S.W. Built 1850 and now derelict, it was the home of merchant industrialist Ewen Wallace Cameron, descendant of the Camerons of Lochiel, partner of Thomas Sutcliffe Mort, vice president of Sydney Hospital and leading Balmain citizen.

Colonnaded verandah of the Mint Building, Macquarie Street, Sydney (designer unknown). Originally the south wing of Macquarie's "Rum Hospital," building commenced in 1810 to replace the "ruinous and unfit" hospital at Dawes Point. Macquarie financed construction by allowing the merchant/contractors, Blaxcell, Riley and D'Arcy Wentworth, a three-year monopoly in the importation of spirits. None of these gentlemen had any previous connections with building but they did have extensive knowledge of the rum trade.

Customs House, Rockhampton, Queensland. The area was first settled in the 1850's; Rockhampton was declared a municipality in 1860 — one of the earliest in Queensland.

Macquarie Fields House, Ingleburn, N.S.W., was built for John Hosking, first Mayor of Sydney.

The Observatory, Sydney, stands on the hill above Dawes Point, site of Governor Phillip's first fort. Observatory Hill housed the public windmills that ground the colony's first grain and for almost a century sprouted flagstafts whose signals alerted the town to the arrival of ships in the harbour. The main building, with domes and tower, was begun in 1857 for Government Astronomer Rev. W. Scott, and the transit of Venus in 1874 was successfully observed here.

Aerial showing the towers and turrets of Government House, Sydney. Stating that "no private gentleman in the colony is so ill-accommodated as I am" in 1817 Governor Macquarie commissioned Francis Greenway to design, in the Gothic style, a "commodious castellated house for the residence of the Governor-in-Chief of the colony". However it was viewed in England as an unnecessary extravagance and construction was halted. Because of the inadequacies of the Sydney residence, the early Governors preferred to use the house at Parramatta. In 1836 work was recommenced (to the design of London architect Edward Blore in the Gothic Revival style) and was completed in 1845.

Conservatorium of Music, Botanic Gardens, Sydney. Built in 1817 as the Government Stables, this was the only part of Greenway's design for Government House that got past the drawing board. The stables remained as such until they were converted into the Conservatorium of Music, in 1916, just a year short of a century after they were built.

The Krait, renowned unit of the Z Force of
World War II, now repaired and moored at
Pittwater, near Sydney, N.S.W. A captured
Japanese fishing vessel, it was used to carry
volunteer Australian and British commandos
in many daring raids. The Krait's most
famous mission was the attack on Japanese
shipping in Singapore Harbour in September,
1943. Forty thousand tonnes of shipping was
destroyed. In the years after the war the
Krait was neglected and allowed to fall into
decay but it has recently been repaired.

Gun battery on Thursday Island, part of the
chain of defensive installations scattered
around the coast and islands of Australia,
results of two World Wars.

defenders...

Though the Commonwealth of Australia had been
inaugurated in 1901 it was not until the Great War of
1914–18 that Australia came of age in the eyes of many.
That holocaust unified the country and gave its people a
sense of nationhood. Her fighting men had travelled half a
world to join the "Motherland" in a war from which the
only possible reward could be honour and glory;
Australians watched their performance with pride and
patriotism. By the end of the war 330,000 men had
embarked for overseas service, over 59,000 of whom did
not return — an appallingly high loss for a country whose
population in 1918 was barely five million. Five of these
men died in a brief battle off Australia's northern shores
— the occupation of German New Guinea; apart from
this, World War I had been fought far from Australian soil
around issues that in no way involved Australia and
against forces that presented no possible threat to her.
It was a different story a generation later, as the battles of
World War II erupted in the Pacific and edged closer to
Australian shores. For the first time in the history of the
land enemy attacks became a reality; a century and a half
of guarding, worrying and fortifying against reflected
threats from Europe came to fruition in 1942 in the face of
a real threat from Asia. Darwin and Broome were
attacked and bombed with heavy losses of life, aircraft
and naval vessels. Australia was ringed by conquered
countries and a hostile ocean. Coastal shipping off New
South Wales and Victoria was constantly sunk by enemy
action. Sydney was shelled and a midget "sub" entered
the harbour; Fort Denison, prepared in the face of a
"Russian threat" a century before received its first war
wound, a crack in its massive stone walls! The smaller
northern towns of Derby and Wyndham were also raided
and an exodus of men, women and children streamed
south. With so many of her men once again fighting in
Europe, Australia now felt her very existence was in peril.
In the belief that an invasion was imminent, a "last ditch"
defence line was traced from Brisbane along the Darling
River to Adelaide (the "Brisbane Line"). This was the
climate in which the great air and naval battles of the
Coral Sea were fought — battles which lessened the
direct threat to Australia although her men in eastern
New Guinea were still engaged in some of the bitterest
fighting of the war.

Scene of the Japanese prisoner of war escape attempt, near Cowra, N.S.W. These peaceful fields witnessed a massacre at dawn on the 5th of August, 1944, when Japanese prisoners of war from the camp here staged a mass outbreak. Over a thousand prisoners, armed with baseball bats and similar makeshift weapons, with blankets and great coats wrapped around them as protection against the barbed wire, made a desperate and tragic bid for freedom. Two hundred and thirty four Japanese were killed and those who succeeded in reaching the surrounding countryside were recaptured within nine days. Three Australian guards were killed. A baseball bat is no match for a rifle.

Jungle around Gove, Arnhem Land, claims a crashed Hudson bomber of World War II. Wreckage of planes such as this, both Japanese and Allied, are scattered in remote areas of the Northern Territory. They are used as a source of metal by nomadic Aborigines, to fashion spear heads and fishing hooks, and regarded in the same light as, say, a stand of trees suitable for spear shafts — as a tribal asset, carefully preserved and visited when the occasion warrants.

Mareeba airstrip near Cairns, Queensland, was a hive of activity in the Battle of the Coral Sea when Australian and American squadrons thwarted the Japanese attack on Port Moresby and Australia in May 1942, inflicting the first defeat on the southward moving force. The large airstrips of that time are now farmlands and only memorials and the remains of an occasional crashed plane serve as reminders of past intensity.

Memorial to the lives lost during the Japanese air raid on Broome in 1942. Sixteen flying boats rode at peace that sunny morning on the waters of Roebuck Bay; they had arrived from Java during the night with Dutch women and children evacuated in the face of the Japanese advance on the Dutch East Indies. Broome had no air defence and each flying boat was systematically destroyed. The war cemetery on the beach contains graves of the seventy victims.

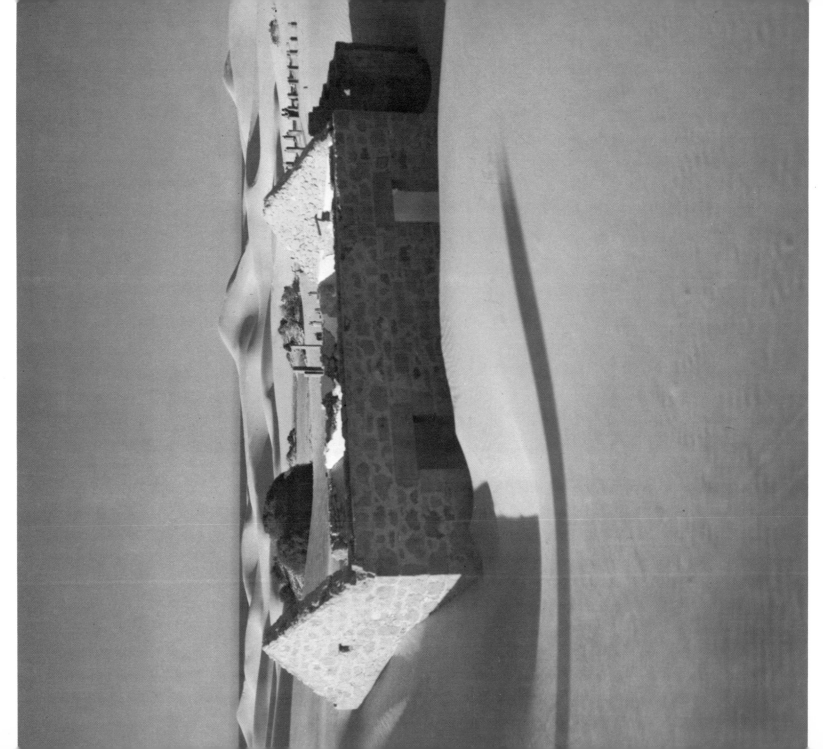

Drifting sands swallow the ruins of the old cable station at Eucla, W.A., an outpost on the shores of the Great Australian Bight. The site was named by explorer E.J. Eyre who found a waterhole nearby on his overland journey around the Bight in 1841. It became a busy and important traffic centre in the 1870's when a repeating telegraph station linking Adelaide and Perth was built. The opening of the telephone link along the Trans-continental railway in 1929 doomed the town to obscurity amidst the dunes.

Battlers

*Remember Thunderbolt, buried under the air raid
trenches;
Remember the bearded men, singing of exile.
Remember the shepherds under their strange stars.*
—Judith Wright

Battler is a peculiarly Australian term for one who struggles against adversity, against the odds. Australian folk memories venerate the battler and the part he has played in our history. Australian folk language commemorates the part he has played in our history. Anzacs at Gallipoli were "Diggers", a name inherited from the men of Eureka, glorious in defeat in an earlier battle. "As game as Ned Kelly" is a term of admiration. The ranks of the battlers include convicts who saw years of work devastated by drought, flood and fire, miners toiling for their elusive pot of gold and the fatalistic "wild colonial boys" who could find no place for themselves within the law but drew grudging admiration for their life outside it, even from their victims. From these came the folk heroes who eclipse many of history's more important names.

The Ballarat gold diggers, badgered and hounded by the "traps" (police) for mining licences and indignant at other injustices, erected a stockade near the Eureka lead on Sunday December 3rd, 1854. Here, with their leader Peter Lalor they swore "by the Southern Cross to stand truly by each other, and fight to defend our rights and liberties". The men who hoisted the flag of the Southern Cross were a mixture of nationalities and represented a cross section of society — but life on the fields was a social leveller. High born and labourer worked together, equalised by the dust. It was the gold licence issue and the vicious "digger-hunts" for those who could not afford one, which placed 150 miners behind the barricades, but their grievances included discontent over corrupt law enforcement, lack of opportunity to purchase land (it was monopolised by wealthy squatting interests) and the right to vote. In view of the high price of their mining licences, the miners felt they were justified in these demands. In the brief and bloody battle which followed, thirty diggers and four soldiers were killed — "martyrs in the cause of liberty". Poet Henry Lawson called it "twenty minutes that freed Australia". American Mark Twain said of it: "I think it may be called the finest thing in Australasian history. It was a revolution — small in size but great politically; it was a strike for liberty, a struggle for a principle, a stand against injustice and oppression."

Ned Kelly, most notorious of all Australian bushrangers, was a battler — against poverty, injustice and persecution. A most articulate, though self-educated man, he outlined his many grievances in his famous "Jerilderie Letter" which he wrote when his gang held the town of Jerilderie captive for two days in 1879. This was the occasion on which he robbed the bank not only of money, but of deeds and mortgages too, and made a bonfire of them in an attempt to benefit people who were in the bank's debt.

Cells at Silverton, west of Broken Hill, N.S.W. Silverton (originally Umberumberka — the change is attributed to a Government official who found the original too hard to spell) was once a flourishing silver-lead mining town with a boom population of three thousand in the 1880's. Its decline began with the development of Broken Hill and it is now a ghost town.

Old gold prospector turned farmer at Alectown, N.S.W., a goldmining centre now almost deserted stands outside the general store once crowded with miners' tools of trade — panning dishes, picks and shovels. Alectown is typical of the many boom towns which grew and disappeared with the gold rushes.

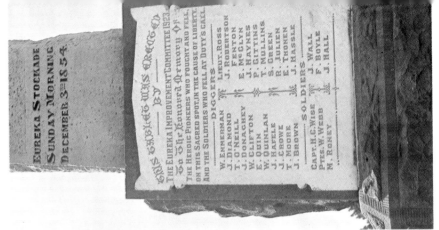

Old buildings at Beechworth, Victoria, boom town of the goldmining era where once the local candidate for Parliament rode through the town on a horse shod with gold won from the local soil.

Drinking fountain at Kalgoorlie, W.A., memorial to Paddy Hannan who discovered the Golden Mile there in 1893. The discovery was a lucky accident — he found a small nugget after his horse lost a shoe — but Paddy never made a fortune from his find.

"In spite of what I'm told, I'm off to search for gold" sang the rainbow-chasers in the days when the Palmer was a river of gold and bullion by the ton was weighed on these scales at the Cooktown bank.

" . . . And the Palmer we will see, my boys, And Cooktown's muddy shore, Where I've been told there's lots of gold, So stay down south no more!"

Names of miners and soldiers who fought and fell at the Eureka Stockade, Sunday 3rd December 1854 are carved on this obelisk to their memory. Thirty diggers and four soldiers were killed — "martyrs in the cause of liberty".

Ruins of administrative buildings at Milparinka, an old mining town in the parched northwest of New South Wales.

Men of the past stand in front of a slab hut in an old goldmining town — one drove the Cobb and Co. coaches, the other was a gold prospector. Both are now farmers.

rainbow chasers...

Gold! "Put it away or we shall all have our throats cut!" shouted Governor Gipps, fearful of the effects of a gold rush on a convict colony. It was a secret which could not be kept for long and it broke in the golden 'fifties. The population grew threefold in a decade and the country was set on a new course. "In spite of what I'm told, I'm off to search for gold!" sang the rainbow-chasers as they rushed in their thousands from all parts of the colony and indeed the globe. Jobs, shops and ships were deserted and the roads to the diggings thronged with a moving mass of hopeful diggers. Tent towns came into being almost as quickly as a new strike.

This unsettling of the settlement was viewed with gloom in some quarters: "The whole non-gold-seeking community was put to great inconvenience, when servants and labour went off to the fields. . . ." "Masters were seen driving their own drays and ladies of great respectability and ample means were obliged to cook the family dinner," bemoaned contemporary observers. And another: "My dear — We are ruined! No more water-hole digging, no more fencing, no more of the usual employment of a social pastoral country . . . All the servants and apprentices have gone."

There was little point in class distinctions on the gold fields. A man was as good as his luck, and life was a quicksilver existence. Diggers with flagging spirits were constantly confronted with stories of fabulous finds,

Lavishly decorated interior of a Chinese joss house, Cooktown, Queensland, is a reminder of the Palmer goldrush days when the Chinese outnumbered the European diggers by the thousands (in 1877 there were 17,000 Chinese and 14,000 Europeans).

Japanese pearl divers' cemetery at Broome, W.A., centre of the world's largest pearling grounds. Cyclonic conditions on the north west coast have taken an enormous toll of lives among the divers and bodies recovered lie buried in this cemetery.

Mining equipment abandoned when production stopped in 1914 — Booengora, near Wellington, N.S.W.

nuggets dug up like a crop of potatoes, but such fortune was by far the exception — a digger was lucky if he could grub enough gold dust to feed himself. Many soon found it easier to get gold from the diggers than from the ground. Some turned shopkeeper; a number exchanged picks for pistols, finding a more rewarding gold yield on the roads.

The roaring days of gold added a new dimension to the Australian scene and the polygot influx which trebled Australia's population inevitably brought both excitement and conflict. They brought new ideas which rocked the foundations of the rigid colonial society — men from Chartist England and rebels from the Californian gold fields. They brought racial tension and for the first time the cry of "White Australia!" was raised as the miners watched with distrust which grew to fever pitch, Chinese fossickers, with their strange appearance and alien culture, working and surviving on deserted "tailings".

Boom towns mushroomed overnight on the diggings. "About a month ago some new diggings were discovered near my run," reads a contemporary account of a strike near Maryborough, Queensland, in 1854, "which have since increased in population at such a rapid rate as to muster now about 15,000 or 20,000. What a month or six weeks ago was a secluded bush valley is now a street about two miles long, lined on both sides with tents of storekeepers, butchers, doctors, barbers, eating houses, refreshments sellers, auctioneers and a host of nondescript tradesmen and etc. too numerous to mention, and with thousands of diggers in the background on both sides ..." Many of these towns no longer exist. Others, their streets lined with relics of the rush, live in the shadow of their former bustling glory and turn to other trades for their livelihood. Beechworth, Victoria, where once the local candidate for parliament rode through the town on a horse shod with gold won from the local soil, now relies on the timber industry for its prosperity.

Rubies, sapphires, jasper and diamonds were once mined there as well as gold, and Beechworth is seeped in the rashness and revelry of the mid-nineteenth century. Ned Kelly spent a time in prison here and his accomplice, Joe Byrne, who died in the Glenrowan shootout, was the son of a Beechworth miner.

Convent at Cooktown, Queensland, where singer Gladys Moncrieff received her early education. Cooktown, Queensland's most northerly town, had a peak population of 30,000 in the 1880's when the Palmer goldfields were in full production; its permanent population now is around three hundred.

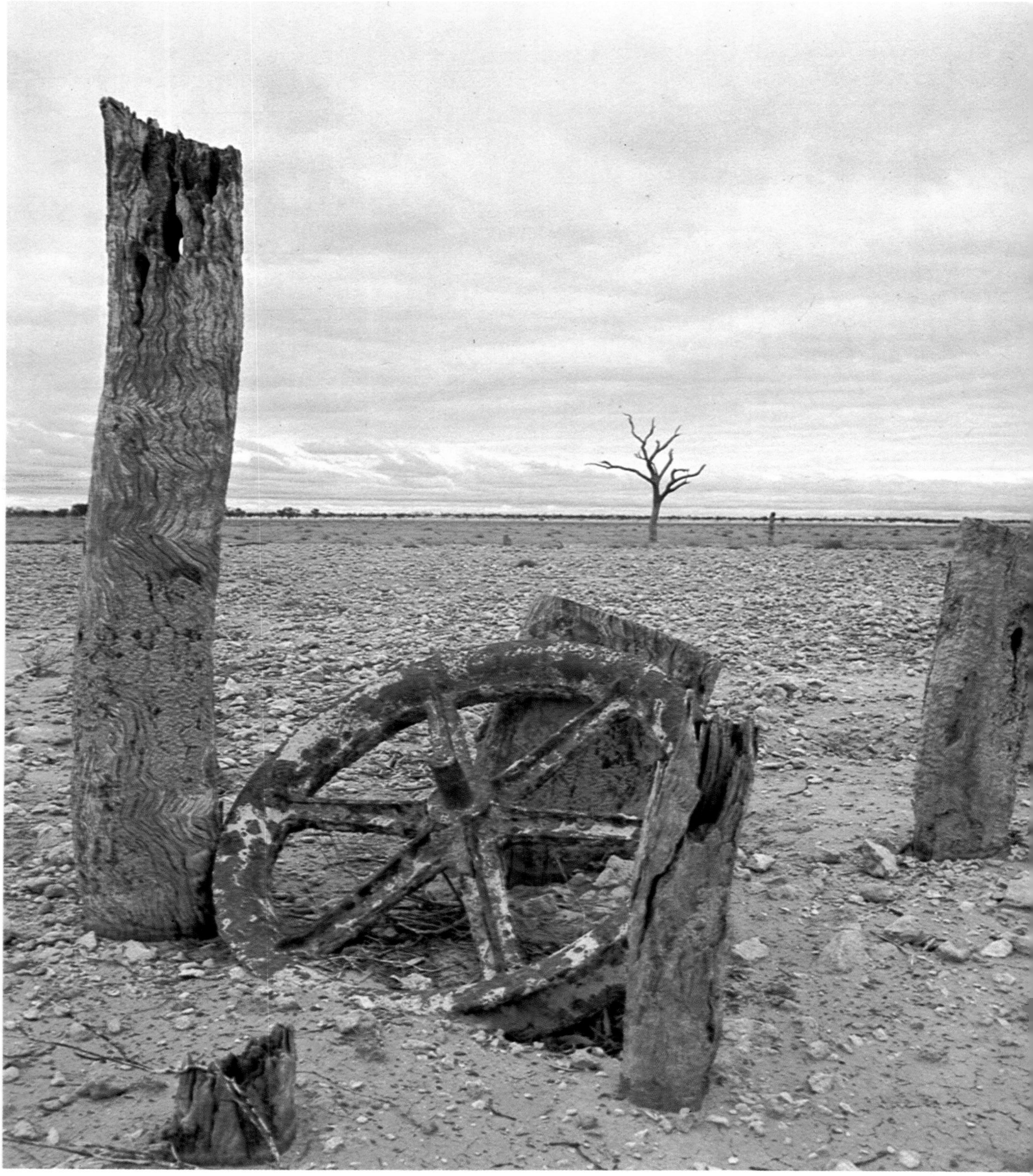

Stark relic of a battle lost, forgotten and decaying on the dry plains near Fort Grey, Queensland. Sturt established a depot near here in 1845 before pressing westward to the salty waters of Lake Blanche and the stony desert which now carries his name. When he returned to Fort Grey he found the depot had been abandoned due to the failure of its water supply.

Port Campbell, Victoria, scene of many shipwrecks. One romantic tale concerns two survivors, a sailor and the young girl he gallantly saved from the sea. Contemporary reports stressed that they slept in separate caves while awaiting rescue!

Seaman's hut, near the summit of Mount Kosciusko, N.S.W. This stone shelter was built as a memorial to a young American, Laurie Seaman, who perished nearby in a blizzard in 1928. It is a survival hut, checked regularly by Park rangers in winter and kept stocked with emergency food and supplies.

unwary...

Emboldened by the success in taming sections of the eastern coast, men grew reckless. Perhaps this land — any part of it — could be conquered. It was there for the taking; all that was needed were orders from above and perseverance from below. Parties set out unprepared for the hazards they were to face — unfamiliar hazards of tropical jungle and endless miles of drifting sands.

Settlements were established and if endeavour, endurance and determination meant anything, they should succeed. In such high hopes were many outposts founded only to flounder in isolated bewilderment.

The first attempt at settlement in the far north of Australia was at Port Essington, on Cobourg Peninsula, the northwest corner of Arnhem Land. Actually, two attempts were made — the first in 1824, when a party was landed and took formal possession in the name of the British Crown; it was abandoned three days later when the party failed to find adequate fresh water. Alternative sites the would-be colonists shifted to, at Fort Dundas, Melville Island, and nearby Raffles Bay on the Cobourg Peninsula, were also abandoned after a somewhat longer stay. But British interest in Australia's northern shores, inspired by the need for a trading post independent of the Dutch and spurred by fears of French settlement, did not lapse. The plan for Port Essington, considered one of the world's finest harbours, was revived, and a second attempt to establish a settlement, sixteen miles inland, was made in 1834. Named Victoria after the Queen and hailed as the future centre of a vast system of commerce with India and Malaya, it was surveyed into town and suburban allotments and settled by Cornishmen who built their stone fireplaces in the humid heat of the tropics. But the hoped for trade which would have made Victoria a wealthy commercial port failed to materialise; the town was off the major trade routes. It was abandoned eleven years later and now all that remains of its existence are a few blackened chimneys and lonely gravestones.

Another ill-fated attempt to establish a major trading centre in Australia's north was made by John Jardine in 1863 at Somerset, near Albany Passage on Australia's northernmost tip, Cape York Peninsula. Ostensibly a pearling centre and harbour of refuge for castaways, it was hoped it would grow into a trading port rivalling Singapore. Jardine built himself a Governor's residence, the town was planned, roads built and allotments sold to speculators in London. All that was needed were settlers but they were not forthcoming. Somerset remained a lonely and isolated pearling station, visited infrequently by passing ships — though it did give succour to the victims of several shipwrecks.

Cobourg Peninsula, the approach to the lonely outpost of Port Essington, scene of a courageous but unsuccessful attempt in 1838 to establish a northern port which would make British traders independent of the Dutch. Named Victoria after the Queen, and hailed as the future centre of a vast system of commerce with India and Malaya, it was settled by Cornishmen who built their stone fireplaces in the humid heat of the tropics, and abandoned eleven years later.

Blackened chimney stands in the solitude of Port Essington, one of the few remaining signs of the ambitious settlement, apart from several lonely graves.

Somerset, near Albany Passage on Cape York Peninsula, the northernmost area of Australia. Today virtually uninhabited it was the scene of an ambitious attempt in 1863 to found a trading port rivalling Singapore. The settlement was harassed by local Aborigines, dogged by a difficult climate and doomed by the rip tide in the Albany Passage which made it a dangerous anchorage.

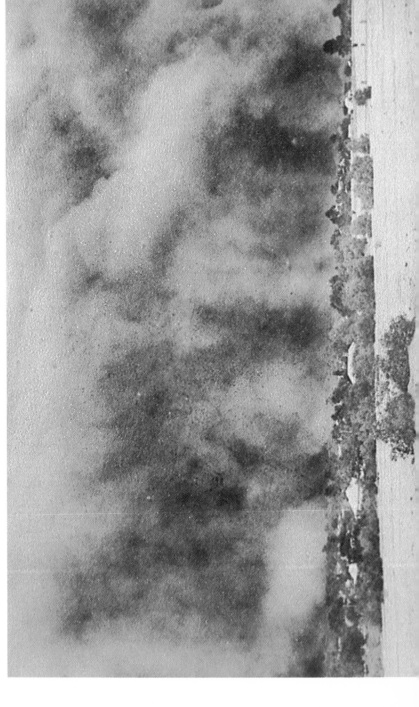

St Stephen's Church, Camperdown, N.S.W., designed by Blacket and built in 1849. Its cemetery contains the graves of the victims of the Dunbar, wrecked near the entrance to Sydney Heads in 1857 with the loss of one hundred and twenty-one lives. There was only one survivor and the bodies of the unidentified dead were buried in a common grave. It was an occasion of great grief in Sydney. Thousands lined the funeral route, business was suspended for the day and ships in port flew flags at half mast. Bodies continued to be washed ashore after the funeral, and one lies buried near Manly beach.

Graves of Aborigines and early settlers on Flinders Island, Bass Strait. When the sealers came to the islands of Bass Strait no native people lived there, but in the 1830's Flinders Island became home to the tragic remnants of the Tasmanian Aborigines who were exiled there after the Black Wars which reduced their numbers to less than two hundred.

Old photograph of a dust storm, one of the many unimagined hazards faced by early settlers in a hostile and unfathomable land.

Cape Wickham lighthouse and the graves of Captain Barnscombe and the crew of the Loch Leven, iron clipper ship wrecked at King Island, Bass Strait, in 1871. The island earned a grim reputation as a graveyard of ships — sixty were lost there in less than half a century with a death toll of over two thousand lives. The western side was last port for many Sydney and Melbourne bound ships; the cutter Tartar went down in 1835 and was followed almost immediately by the convict transport Neva with a loss of 215 lives. In 1845 the barque Cataraqui was lost with 406 lives; she had been carrying emigrants for Melbourne. More fortunate were those on another emigrant ship, the Netherby bound for Brisbane, wrecked in 1866. All 450 aboard were saved and were cared for by the lighthouse keeper at Cape Wickham until assistance arrived. They must surely have strained available resources!

The Gap, Watsons Bay, N.S.W., scene of the tragic wreck of the Dunbar in 1857. On the stormy night of the 20th August the Dunbar inched her way from Botany Bay to Port Jackson; near Sydney Heads visibility became so bad that all sight of land was lost. A popular theory is that the captain mistook the Gap for the entrance to Sydney Harbour but it is more likely he was driven ashore by the strong easterly gale. Wreckage and bodies were washed ashore on the beaches of Middle and North Harbours for many days after the tragedy.

Memorial to Mrs Watson, heroine of the Lizard Island tragedy, stands in the main street of Cooktown. The inscription reads:

Five fearful days beneath the scorching glare
Her babe she nursed.
God knows the pangs the woman had to bear,
Whose last sad entry showed a mother's care —
"Near dead with thirst".

Lizard Island, about sixty miles north east of Cooktown, where Mary Watson lived with her husband, a bêche de mer fisherman, and infant son. On 27th September 1881 while the husband was away seeking new fishing grounds, the Watson home was attacked by Aborigines. One of their two Chinese servants was killed and the other wounded before the attackers were driven off by shots from Mrs Watson. Mary herself was wounded. "I got three spears from them," she wrote in the tragic diary which she kept throughout the dreadful days that followed. As the natives remained in the vicinity, she decided to escape by sea. The only thing they could find for the attempt was an iron tank, four feet by four feet, used for boiling bêche de mer. In this unwieldy vessel she, her baby and the Chinese servant made an incredible voyage, eventually landing on an island forty-odd miles away after paddling for several days. Unfortunately they could find no water on the island, and all three died there of thirst. Their bodies were not discovered until a chance visit to the island three months later, when they were taken to Cooktown and buried there. The iron tank in which they travelled is now in the Queensland Museum, Brisbane, and the diary in which she recorded the events of those eleven days is in the Oxley Memorial Library, also in Brisbane. The last entry reads: "No rain. Morning fine weather. Ah Sam preparing to die. Have not seen him since 9. Ferrier more cheerful. Self not feeling at all well. Have not seen any boat of any description. No water. Nearly dead with thirst."

Grave of Mary Watson at Cooktown, Qld.

Ruins of the Watson house on Lizard Island. It was constructed of blocks of coral cut from the nearby reef.

In Memory of
Mrs WATSON
HEROINE OF
LIZARD ISLAND TRAGEDY OF 1881.

AND HER INFANT SON FERRIER.

Who built and laboured here?
The wind and the sea say
—Their cold nest is broken
and they are blown away.

They did not breed nor love.
Each in his cell alone
cried as the wind now cries
through this flute of stone.

These lines from Judith Wright's
The Old Prison capture the futility and
desolation of the ruins of convict penal
settlements scattered in various places
in Australia. Pictured above are the convict
ruins at Kingston, Norfolk Island, a place of
"extremest punishment short of death",
administered savagely in the shadow of the
gallows. At right are the ruins of the terrible
Lynton gaol, a convict hiring station near
Port Gregory, W.A. During the brief period of
transportation to Western Australia hiring
stations such as this were established to
provide labour to work on private farms.

Convict-built tunnel carved through solid
rock on the old and virtually disused Glen
Innes/Grafton road.

Convict hiring station at Lynton, W.A. —
flour mill and commander's residence.

unwilling...

Without the lash-driven labour of Australia's earliest and unwilling migrants the settlement at Sydney Cove could not have survived. The brutal transportation system provided the colony with a workforce without which roads and bridges could not have been built, land could not have been cleared and cultivated. As Australian poet Mary Gilmore expressed it for them in *Old Botany Bay:* "I bore the heat, I blazed the track — Furrowed and bloody upon my back. I split the rock; I felled the tree: The nation was — Because of me!" Herded and beaten like animals the convicts were forced first to build their own gaols and then to erect towns around them. Though few were masons, brickmakers, architects or builders, between them they constructed many fine buildings. An admission of the vital role played by the convicts in the founding of Australia came from the colony of Swan River, Western Australia. Founded in 1829 as a place for free men, removed from the stigma of a penal settlement, it grew to envy the captive convict labour of the east and in 1849 petitioned the British Government for convicts to build roads and other public works and be available for farm labour. The British Government, its gaols still overflowing, welcomed the proposal. The first batch of convicts arrived soon after, in 1850. These convicts had VG (Very Good) and G (Good) stencilled on their sleeves — the cream of the gaols had been sent! Roads and public buildings materialised; convict hiring stations were built in country areas from which convicts could be hired for work on farms. This hiring was seasonal, and when the men were not wanted for harvest or seeding they worked on community projects.

Sealed roads stretched over the hills and into the farming areas where before there were only sand tracks. Wells were sunk at intervals. The general condition of the colony improved rapidly. There were fewer unskilled convicts and only those with good records were sent, all of them too near their tickets-of-leave to want to escape. Transportation in Western Australia lasted eighteen years, from 1850 to 1868. Ironically the last years were marked by a complete reversal of the benign approach to the transported labour which had put the colony on its feet. When the British Government gave notice of their decision to stop transportation the Governor of the day was a former Tasmanian, Dr Hampton. He determined to make the most of the last years and speed up construction of roads. Discipline became incredibly severe and prisoners in leg irons worked under the lash. Escape attempts were common but rarely successful, and recaptured convicts were lashed and spent months in solitary confinement or years on the roads in irons.

St Bernard's Church and Presbytery, Hartley, N.S.W. Built in 1842 it played an important role in the lives of the predominantly Irish Catholic local population. These buildings are directly opposite the Hartley Courthouse. Hartley village (known as the "Vale of Clwyd" prior to 1838) is now an historic site under the protection of the National Parks and Wildlife Service.

Hangman's Rock, Wiseman's Ferry, N.S.W. Legend has it that this formed a natural gallows. Convicts are said to have been hanged here — dropped through the hole in the rock.

Guards' House, Hartley. A large convict population was centred around Hartley in the 1830's; some engaged in the building of Victoria Pass and some assigned as labourers to local settlers.

Ruins of the penal settlement at Trial Bay, on the mouth of the Macleay River, N.S.W. Building was started in 1876. It was to house convicts engaged in building a breakwater on the bay and was also seen as a reformatory for long term prisoners. The building, with walls eighteen feet high and eighteen inches thick, took its first complement of prisoners in 1886. Work on the breakwater was abandoned in 1903 and the gaol closed, although it saw a further period of use during World War I when German internees were confined there. A memorial which they erected to their dead was blown up by patriotic locals. In 1922 the gaol was closed, all removable parts were sold and only ruined rows of unroofed cells remain. Trial Bay gets its name from the brig Trial, which was stolen by convicts in 1816 and sailed north to the mouth of the Macleay River, where it was wrecked.

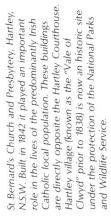

Post Office, Jerilderie, N.S.W. In 1879 Ned Kelly and his gang held up the town for two days and robbed the bank of £2000.

This bullet, fired by bushranger Morgan at Lockhart, N.S.W., was removed from the body of police magistrate Bayliss. Bayliss lived to tell the tale and wear the gold-mounted bullet on his watch chain.

The grave of Ben Hall, Forbes, N.S.W. "An outcast from society, he was forced to take to the road" sings the old colonial ballad. The tombstone reads: "In memory of Ben Hall Shot 5th May 1865 Aged 27 years"

Thunderbolt's grave (Fred Ward) Uralla, N.S.W. He was thirty when he was killed in 1870.

bolters and bushrangers...

"Poor Ben Hall, he had a property of his own, near Forbes, and all the bad deeds that used to be done were pinned onto poor Ben Hall. He was yarding his cattle this day and they come onto him and took him into Forbes for trial for something that he didn't do, and all his cattle were left in the yard. Instead of the police pulling the sliprails down and letting them out, they was all left to perish.

"And when he came out after doing a month in jail they were just carcasses in the yard. They burned his place down. His wife betrayed him and went off with another man. Ben took to the bush then and turned out to be a highwayman." So reads a contemporary account of Ben Hall, a perfect example of the "romantic" bushranger, who was regarded by a large section of the public — and quite a few of the police — as a man of decency and kindness. He died in a hail of police bullets in May 1865. The tracker, Billy Dargen, shot and wounded Hall, who begged: "Finish me, Billy. Rather you than the traps." Dargen's next bullet went through his head, killing him, but his body was then riddled with bullets (reports vary from fifteen to thirty) from the police who left their hiding places to shoot him as he fell. Dargen and Ben Hall had known each other since childhood. The black tracker apparently had no particular feelings of either animosity or loyalty, but saw his job as a job.

Ben Hall was born in 1837, the son of two convicts. His father was a West Countryman, transported for stealing a handkerchief, and his mother an Irish girl. These two were pioneers of the Lachlan River district, where they raised their family, and when at the age of twenty-three Ben Hall had his first encounter with police, he had already established his own cattle run — 600 head — on a property in the Weddin Mountains. Hall was arrested on what proved to be a false charge, spent some weeks in gaol awaiting a trial

Port Arthur, dreaded place of secondary punishment on sea-locked Tasman Peninsula, was feared by convicts as a place of "unmitigated wretchedness" and regarded by the authorities as remote enough to deter escape. Nevertheless conditions there were so harsh that many attempted to do so, some successfully. These were the "bolters", from bolters to bushrangers is a logical step and Van Diemen's Land gaol of the twice-convicted, produced some of the most violent as well as some of the boldest and most daring. Lower picture of the magazine tower, shows the skilled masonry that was a feature of the buildings.

Pioneers' graves at Tibooburra, N.S.W. stand forlorn, claimed by the bleak dry land they never really conquered. A child's cot marks a small grave. The despair of those settlers who faced failure in the west is captured in the lines of Henry Lawson:

The crops have withered from the ground,
The tank's clay bed is glarin',
But from my heart no tear nor sound,
For I have got past carin'. . . .
Through Death and Trouble, turn about,
Through hopeless desolation,
Through flood and fever, fire and drought,
And slavery and starvation;
Through childbirth, sickness, hurt and blight,
And nervousness and scarin',
Through being left alone at night,
I've come to be past carin'.

Tibooburra is in the area explored by Sturt in 1844. The name means "heap of granite".

Pioneer woman of the west, Mrs Andrews, rode for six months on this waggon, from Port Lincoln, South Australia, to Alice Springs. Those who ventured into the dry interior following the lure of gold — fleece or wheat or ore — were a hard and stubborn people. Things rarely came easily and rarely did they give in easily. Those that they laid grudgingly under the hard dry dirt tied them even more tenaciously to the soil — for a part of themselves was now a part of the land. They had planted their own flesh and blood and wanted the harvest.

at which he was promptly acquitted, and returned to find his wife had run away with a former policeman, taking their young son with her. A few weeks later he was again arrested, this time perhaps with more cause, but was not brought to trial and was eventually released. It was during this second period that his stock died and his homestead was razed by police. He sold the run for a pittance and took to the bush.

For the next three years Hall and his gang carried out a series of well-planned and daring raids. They were not bloodthirsty — Hall was responsible for no-one's death — and were not particularly money-hungry, either. When the gang held up the town of Canowindra they staged a three-day party for the townspeople, using the proceeds of their robberies and more to pay the publican for all grog and grub consumed and leaving poorer than when they came. Ben Hall had many sympathisers among the poorer settlers and bush workers of the Lachlan, and few there were who would begrudge him hospitality — though they preferred he keep out of sight. His death caused much lamenting:

Pray do not stay your seemly grief
But let a tear-drop fall,
For many hearts shall always mourn
The fate of Bold Ben Hall

No more he'll mount the gallant steed
Nor range the mountains high;
The widow's friend in poverty,
Bold Ben Hall, good bye!

Dreamers

Australia, ancient chimera land shrouded for aeons in myth and fantasy, has long been home to dreamers. For countless centuries the first Australians drifted across the continent, claiming it for their own in the most intimate way, weaving it inextricably into their dreams. To the Aborigine, every part of his tribal territory, every rock, every tree, river and waterhole and mountain, had personality, a name and a story. Outstanding natural features were revered as increase sites, places visited in the Dreamtime by totemic ancestors. Caves and rock shelters, richly decorated with paintings and engravings, were repositories of ritual and mythological history, ceremonial and teaching sites where the Aborigine learned the lessons of the past.

For Aborigines dream of a time beyond memory when the earth was flat and featureless and there were no flowers, no food, no people. Then sometime, somehow, out of the earth or out of the sea, travelling over the edge of the world or descending from the sky, came the creative super-beings. These Dreamtime heroes walked upon the land and decreed what should exist. Gullies appeared where they dug the earth and streams where they urinated. Fleeting of form, they were sometimes human, sometimes animal, sometimes male and sometimes female. They created everything; gave birth to man and the other creatures, changed one another into trees and mountains, flung up the moon and stars that shine in the sky. Everything that moved on earth, everything that grew, everything that had substance and form, was created by these people of the Dreamtime.

'Mother, what make sunset fire,
Every night the big red glare?'
'Biami's gunya out that way,
That his camp fire over there.'
'How come great wide river here,
Where we swim and fish with spear?'
'Biami dug him.
You see big hills all about?
They the stuff that he chuck out.'

Then, mysteriously, the Dreamtime came to an end, and the creative heroes left, sometimes turning themselves into sacred objects, sometimes sinking into a rock face, leaving an impression for men to see and trace with paint. Spirit figures such as these occur in caves throughout the continent, and art is an essential ingredient of Aboriginal life, permeating every aspect, both ceremonial and secular. It is sorcery and magic, and the expression of deeply held religious beliefs, the source of fertility and natural increase, the saga of achievements and the daily record of gossip, hunting, loves and hates.

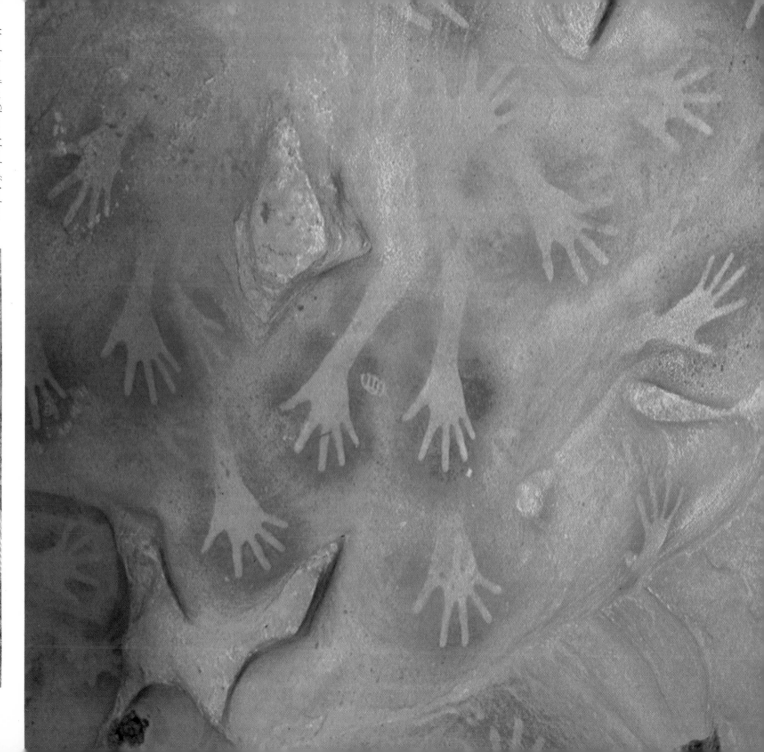

Hand stencils at Chasm Island, off Arnhem Land, Northern Territory, made by blowing powdered red ochre onto a hand (usually the left one) held against the surface of the rock. These cave paintings were recorded by Matthew Flinders in 1803.

Enos Namatjira, eldest son of Aboriginal artist Albert Namatjira carries on his father's tradition under the watchful eye of his dog.

Rock engravings of Baiame the Sky Father and Daramulen his brother/son, creative heroes of the sandstone tribes of Ku-ring-gai, N.S.W.

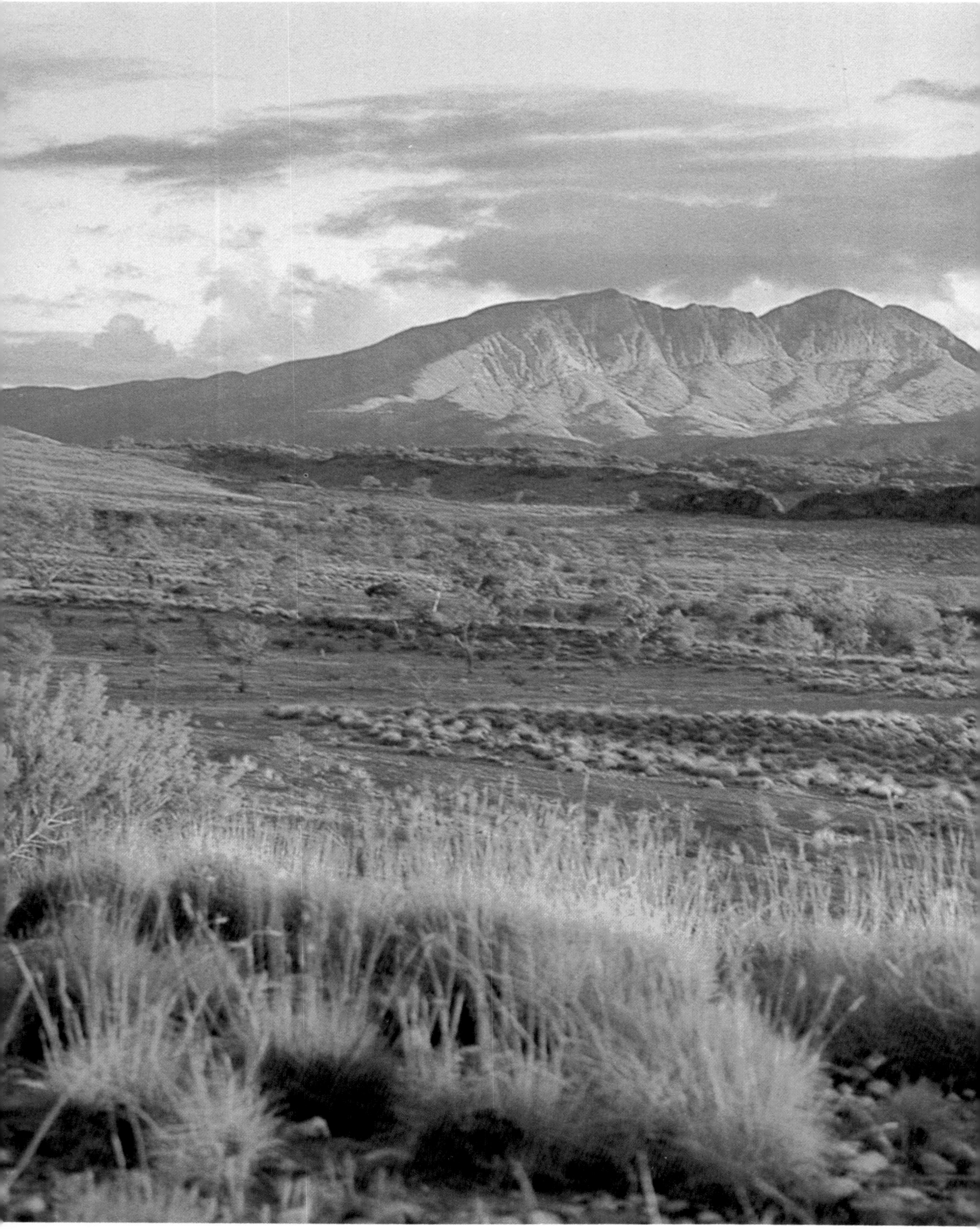

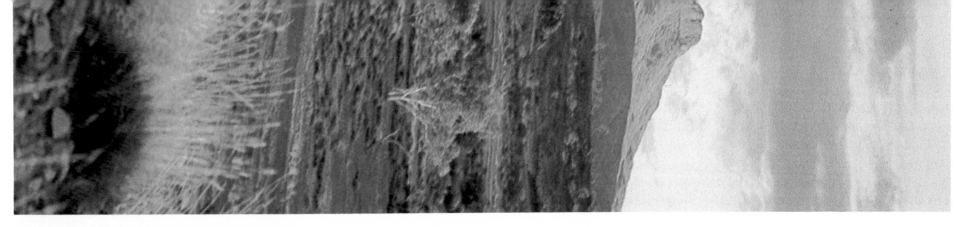

Mount Sonder, central Australia, features prominently in Namatjira paintings. Natural formations have tremendous significance in traditional Aboriginal life—each rock, each tree, has a name and a story.

Aboriginal burial ground, Tibooburra, N.S.W. Like all the races of man, Aborigines regard death with awe and fear, and disposal of the dead is marked by solemn ceremonies. Generally bodies are buried in shallow graves, marked by a mound surmounted with logs or in some cases uprooted trees.

Albert Namatjira lies buried in a "white man's grave"—surrounded by the unmarked mounds of his people—even in death he did not escape the turmoil and tangle of the two worlds which divided his life. He died a broken and disillusioned man not long after his release from Alice Springs gaol where he had served a sentence for illegally supplying liquor to his brethren. He found it difficult to return to painting. "I can't paint yet, still too sad. When I live with my own people again, in my own country, perhaps then I paint." However he seemed to have lost the will to live. The few paintings he attempted in the short time between his release and death were marked by disturbingly harsh colour combinations.

Aboriginal rock stacks near Milparinka, N.S.W. This is possibly an old bora ground — secret site used for initiation ceremonies. Boras consist of two circular areas, one smaller than the other, usually defined by stones. The circles are linked by a path and represent the womb — in all stages of initiation the emphasis is on rebirth.

Pecked intaglios, Mootwingie, N.S.W. Probably the most ancient form of Aboriginal pictorial art, these curious combinations of geometric designs are common in the area. Present-day Aborigines say they were made by the people of the Dreamtime — they know nothing of their meaning or of how they were made.

The Aborigine is instinctively a poet and painter — these are forms of expression inherent in his cultural tradition. It is not so much "art for art's sake" — their languages have no words which correspond exactly with "art" and "artist" though there are terms for the different techniques of painting, carving etc. — but rather a subsidiary element in the whole of life, with no need for a special name. It is used with great purpose in ceremonial rituals, in teaching and the telling of tales. It is also used in the decoration of utilitarian objects — spears, dillybags, didgeridoos. Even the large grinding stones of the women often have designs carved on the undersurface, though these could not be seen unless the heavy mortar was overturned. Singing and dancing is also very much part of traditional Aboriginal life, and the corroboree is an important medium of expression, practised by all — men, women and children alike. Epic tales of hunting and history, mythology and love, are woven into song and music and dance, part of the background of every Aboriginal child from earliest babyhood.

Artist Albert Namatjira carried this tradition into the white man's world. He found himself in a society eager for his paintings yet resolutely unwilling to understand his culture. A man of dignity, intellect and genius, he mirrored in water colour the haunting beauty of his tribal Aranda territory. Trapped between two worlds, his life was a tragic saga of disillusion. Lorded and lampooned, praised and persecuted, exploited by a white society in which he found little tolerance, he died a broken and bewildered fringe-dweller.

Aboriginal man, you walked with pride,
And painted with joy the countryside.
Original man, your fame grew fast.
Men pointed you out as you went past . . . .
What did their loud acclaim avail
Who gave you honour, then gave you jail?
Namatjira, they boomed your art,
They called you genius, then broke your heart.

wrote Australian poet Kath Walker, herself an Aborigine, whose poem *Biami* is quoted on page 126.

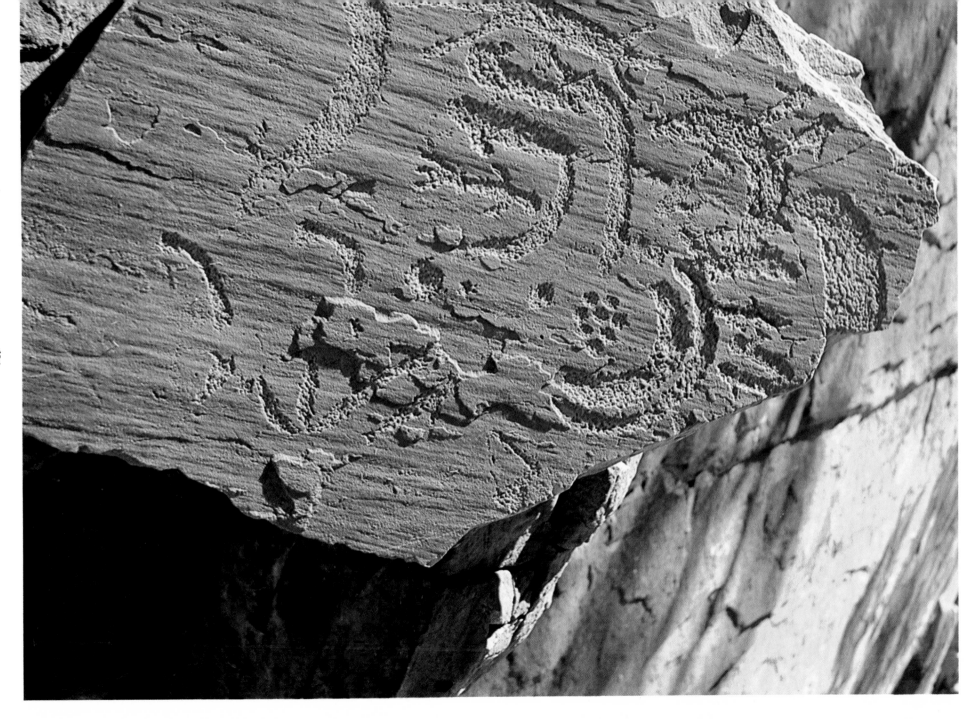

Home of Australian poet, Dorothea Mackellar, stands in tree-flanked seclusion at Lovett's Bay, Pitwater, N.S.W. In "My Country", perhaps her best-known work, she sang of the sunburnt wilful land and she loved.

poets and painters...

Every culture has its artists. Australia is home to a later breed who, though reflecting cultures of other countries, have been touched by the land they seek to interpret and are at one with the poets and painters of the Dreamtime. Artists and draftsmen came with exploring ships and struggled to capture the exotic strangeness of the new land for the eyes of the old world. Painters followed the shearers and gold diggers across a canvas of orange and brown; they explored the cool pastels of the misty valleys and the changing nuances of the changeless bush. A distinctive Australian art style came in the 1880's with Tom Roberts, Arthur Streeton and the group known as the Heidelberg School. Working outdoors, driven by a genuine affection for the Australian bush, they investigated the light and atmosphere of their surroundings and produced the first truly Australian landscapes. Hans Heysen sought the soul of the land in the shape and colour of a gumtree. William Dobell and Russell Drysdale broke sharply with established tradition. Drysdale fled to the scorched umber of the outback where gaunt figures towered from the red dust of an ageless and lonely land; Dobell rejected the image of Australia as desolate desert and depicted the moody shores of Lake Macquarie where he lived much of his life. He created his own form of portraiture and found himself the scapegoat in one of the most bitter controversies in Australian art after his portrait *Joshua Smith* won the Archibald Prize for 1943. The portrait, a major break with academic art tradition, was denounced as "a travesty . . . a gross caricature" and was the subject of an unsuccessful lawsuit by two disgruntled fellow entrants. The prolonged furore so upset Dobell, a sensitive and retiring man, that he retreated to the seclusion of Wangi and it was there, on the shores of Lake Macquarie, that many of his famous paintings were later produced.

Artist Sir William Dobell working on a portrait of Helena Rubenstein at his home at Wangi, Lake Macquarie, N.S.W.

Author Ion Idriess, at 83. His many novels, biographies and short stories, covering colourful and little known aspects of Australia and its history, have had a profound influence on two generations of Australians and their attitude towards their country.

Hans Heysen, who introduced the "gum tree" school of Australian painting, with his dog on his property at Hahndorf, South Australia, among the trees he so lovingly and skilfully portrayed.

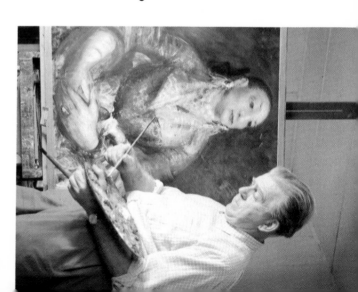

In the tracks of the Aboriginal legend tellers wander the bush balladists, poets and writers of the last two centuries. They travel a pioneering land, a raw and rough-edged country where gold is where you find it and tall tales are often true. Early exiles sang of their homeland and hummed the banned verses of bushranging to lilting Irish airs. The ballads of the bush workers hurled raucous defiance at the squatters. Australian literature is based on the turbulence and unrest of early settlement, the droving, mustering, bullockies and shearers that came with the growth of station life, and the fledgling literary groups which sprang up in the towns and cities. As old literary values adjusted to new conditions in a new environment, as the numbers of Australian-born increased, so there developed a distinctive national outlook. Early poetry was written by Englishmen interpreting the Australian scene through English eyes. Native-born Henry Kendall, whose lyrical poetry was inspired by the scenery of coastal New South Wales, made the first tentative breaks with this tradition. Eureka and the rise of the labour movement, Federation and two world wars, further stimulated a national outlook. 'Banjo' Paterson followed the anonymous bush balladists. Henry Lawson depicted a different and harsher side of rural life; he was part also of the struggle for recognition of Australian artists in their own land: "Till Australian scenes on canvas shall repay the artist's hand, And the songs of southern poets shall be ringing thro' the land", he wrote in his little-known verse, *A Song of Southern Writers*. Australian prose writers shook off the shackles of nineteenth-century English style with greater ease. Early novelists concentrated on simply-told tales of convicts and bushrangers, squatters and settlers. Australia has produced novelists of world reputation, starting with Henry Handel Richardson (Mrs J. G. Robertson) at the turn of the century and culminating with Patrick White, Nobel prizewinner for literature in 1974.

Guthega Dam in the Australian Alps, part of the Snowy Mountains Hydro-Electric Scheme, Australia's greatest engineering undertaking and one of the world's largest irrigation and power projects.

Ord River Project, in Western Australia, where the Ord River, which carries Australia's largest flow of water, has been utilised in a major irrigation and hydro-electric scheme. Plains once used solely for scattered sheep and cattle now support crops of cotton, rice, sugar cane, safflower and linseed.

Montsalvat, part of the artists' colony at Eltham, Victoria. The house was built in 1934 by artist and architect Justus Jorgensen; it is constructed of stone, timber, rammed earth and mud bricks. Eltham is unique for its artists, writers and musicians and the mud-brick homes in which they live.

Interior of Edron, built at Twofold Bay, N.S.W., in 1911 by the Logan family. Like Boyd before them, they dreamed of a vast city there. It is now a holiday guest house.

visionaries...

Australia's shores were washed by waves of dreamers, lured by elusive promises — visionaries who saw cities rising from the untouched bush, men who thrust into the mystifying interior in fruitless searches for an inland sea or spent back-breaking months on the goldfields, ever hopeful of fortune at the next turn of the shovel. Men dreamt of harnessing rivers to water the inland, and planned a new Utopia in a fresh land of opportunity unfettered by the rigid traditions of the old world. Some were to live out their visions; others saw them blighted and distorted. It was a tantalising land for the idealist.

As the first groups of exiles faltered on the shores of Sydney Cove, the dreamers amongst them saw visions in the stretching lands of their prison. Two such men were convict Francis Greenway and Governor Lachlan Macquarie. Greenway, an architect, was transported in 1814 for forging endorsement on a contract. He gained his pardon on completing, in 1817, Australia's first lighthouse, at South Head. Macquarie was a strict military man, a career officer who had served the army in North America, India, Egypt and Europe. Together the architect of Bath and the Highlander from the Hebrides wove dreams to transform the makeshift colony.

Lake Burley Griffin, man-made lake and focal point of Walter Burley Griffin's imaginative design for the city of Canberra which won an international competition in 1912.
However like Greenway before him and Utzon who was to follow, his visions were tangled in red tape and distorted by officialdom. He left his dream city "under protest and with great regret" when responsibility for the city's design and construction was transferred to the Works Department in 1921.

Designed by Burley Griffin as an incinerator, this building in Toowoomba, Queensland, has been preserved and converted to a repertory theatre.

Macquarie Lighthouse, South Head, Sydney. The original lighthouse was built to Francis Greenway's design in 1817. However, because of the use of inferior stone it quickly became unstable. In 1833 a copy of Greenway's lighthouse was built nearby and is still in use today.

Macquarie planned a spacious city. The narrow haphazard streets, traced by the feet of the first settlers seeking the easiest way from place to place, were widened and dignified with Royal names. The city gained many of its distinctive features, best seen today in the 'well-proportioned buildings fringing the northern end of Hyde Park. Had their plans been carried to fruition, Sydney would have had a grand civic square surrounded by gracious buildings. Their dreams were halted by the frugal hand of Mr Commissioner Bigge who could see no reason to glorify a gaol. Plans for a cathedral and new Government House were abandoned, but Greenway managed to complete the Government stables in the castellated Gothic grandeur of the original design. Commissioner Bigge was outraged at this "useless magnificence" and it was suggested to Governor King, who succeeded Macquarie, that it be transformed into the official Government residence. However the stables remained as such until 1916, almost a century after they were built, when they were converted into the present Conservatorium of Music.

After Greenway came two men who trod the same unhappy path. In 1912 Walter Burley Griffin won an international competition for the layout of Australia's capital city; but in realising his dream Griffin plunged headlong into a bitter feud with the Board of Works, which eventually led to a Ministerial Committee of experts taking control of the project. Fifty years later the major buildings which he envisaged as the heart of the capital — Parliament House, the Halls of Justice and the Executive Buildings — have still not been built. A similar fate befell Joern Utzon, designer of the shimmering cluster of shells that nestle by the harbour on Bennelong Point. The project was beset by difficulties; after years of haggling, Utzon felt "forced to resign" and his vision was taken over by an architectural panel. In the festivities and fanfare of the carnival which accompanied the opening of the Sydney Opera House there was one notable absentee in the ranks of celebrities — its creator, Joern Utzon.

138

Mount Warning and the MacPherson Ranges at sunset. The mountain was sighted and named by Cook in his voyage up the coast in 1770. Describing it as a "remarkable sharp peaked Mountain" he gave it its name as a warning to mariners of treacherous reefs encountered in nearby waters. The MacPherson Ranges, which straddle the New South Wales/Queensland border, were the scene of the Stinson air disaster in 1937.

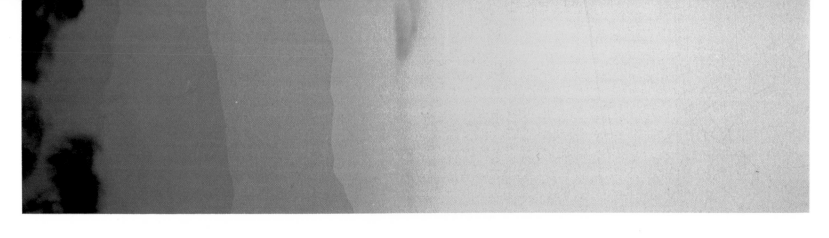

index...

Page numbers in bold type refer to illustrations or captions